GREAT BOOKS FOR CHILDREN

Preeti Singh worked for a number of years in the corporate sector. She is also a voracious reader and is currently working on a novel and a series of books on Indian history for children.

GREAT BOOKS FOR CHILDREN
A Guide

edited and compiled by
PREETI SINGH

RED TURTLE
RUPA

Published in Red Turtle by
Rupa Publications India Pvt. Ltd. 2014
7/16, Ansari Road, Daryaganj
New Delhi 110002

Sales Centres:

Allahabad Bengaluru Chennai
Hyderabad Jaipur Kathmandu
Kolkata Mumbai

Introduction copyright © Preeti Singh 2014
Edition copyright © Rupa Publications India Pvt. Ltd. 2014

All rights reserved.
No part of this publication may be reproduced, transmitted, or stored in a
retrieval system, in any form or by any means, electronic,
mechanical, photocopying, recording or otherwise,
without the prior permission of the publisher.

ISBN: 978-81-291-2366-4

10 9 8 7 6 5 4 3 2 1

Printed in India by Gopsons Papers Ltd., Noida

This book is sold subject to the condition that it shall not,
by way of trade or otherwise, be lent, resold, hired
out, or otherwise circulated, without the publisher's prior consent,
in any form of binding or cover other than that in which it is published.

Contents

Introduction	*vii*
Adventure	1
Crime and Mystery	39
Fantasy	60
Growing Up	89
Historical Fiction and Books on History	117
Humour	142
Manga Comics	156
Science Fiction	163
Supernatural and Horror	188
Traditional Tales	201
Books for Young Readers	211
Evergreen Reads	218

INTRODUCTION

There are books and books and more books. In each book the author creates a world that you can step into, be immersed in, connect with the characters and live the story.

What should you be reading? Actually, no one can tell you what you 'should' or 'must' read. You need to figure that out for yourself. I have read thousands of books since I was a little girl, and I cannot say I have a single favourite book. Each book I loved made a connection with me. They stayed with me in good times and bad, in happy times and sad.

So explore the books that are listed in the following pages. If you are a reader, then you know that books can fit into more than one genre. For the sake of simplicity here, the books have been organized by genres—science fiction, fantasy, adventure, growing up, classics and so on. Other books by the same author have also been listed.

The genres have been divided according into three levels. These refer to the level of reading you might be at. But treat these levels as flexible. Look for books at the level above or below yours too, to find anything that interests you.

Short descriptions outline what the books are about, but don't judge the books by only that. Listen to your instinct, and if a book calls out to you, pick it up to read it!

Preeti Singh

Adventure

Who doesn't love a good adventure story? The protagonist can go on an intergalactic adventure, or a treasure hunt and battle pirates, or get lost while travelling to the centre of the earth—there's nothing that beats settling down with a good adventure book and thinking, if only I could do all that!

The books listed below are about adventures in schools and strange lands, with pirates and wizards, and are sure to enthrall you.

LEVEL 1

KRISTY'S GREAT IDEA • Ann M. Martin
To earn loads of money and have a good time with her friends, Kristy decides to start a baby-sitter's club. What seems like a good idea at first, is not so good after all. Not an easy task managing the terrible twos and trying to keep track of suspicious things around them!

Other books in the Baby-Sitter's Club series:

There are more than 130 books in the series, some of which are:
- The Fire at Mary-Ann's House
- Abby's Un-Valentine
- Claudia and the Phantom Phone Calls
- Other spin-offs from the Baby-Sitter's Club
- The Baby-Sitter's Club Mysteries

The Baby-Sitter's Club Super Mysteries
The Baby-Sitter's Club Super Specials
The Baby-Sitter's Club Little Sister
The Baby-Sitter's Club Little Sister Super Specials
The Baby-Sitter's Club Friends Forever

SWALLOWS AND AMAZONS • Arthur Ransome

Meet the Walker and Blackett children in the period between the two World Wars. The Walkers consider themselves to be explorers and the Blacketts are pirates. Join them in their adventures in their summer holidays in England and Scotland.

Other books in the series:
Swallowdale
Peter Duck
Winter Holiday
Coot Club
Pigeon Post

PIPPI LONGSTOCKING • Astrid Lindgren

Nine-year-old Pippi Longstocking is kind and friendly, but she is unconventional. She grew up on her father's ship and does not tolerate adults who are rude and pompous. She is at her very worst with such people. She has lots of interesting adventures with her friends Tommy and Annika.

Other books in the series
Pippi Goes on Board
Pippi in the South Seas

AMIE AND THE CHAWL OF COLOUR • Chatura Rao

Doombay, Annie's city, has lost all its colour and Annie's mother is sick. In order to save her mother and the city, Amie decides to go and get colour from the Shah of the Hue country. Along the way, she meets a flea, a rat and an ant.

THE ADVENTURES OF CAPTAIN UNDERPANTS • Dav Pilkey

When the principal of their school, Mr Krupp, records George and Harold's pranks on the football team, he threatens to expose them if they will not do his bidding. The boys are forced into Mr Krupp's service until they get a 3-D Hypno-ring to hypnotise Mr Krupp. As Captain Underpants, Mr Krupp is now at the mercy of the two pranksters!

Other books in the Captain Underpants series:

There are nine books in the Captain Underpants series, some of which are:

Captain Underpants and the Attack of the Talking Toilets
Captain Underpants and the Invasion of the Incredibly Naughty Cafeteria Ladies from
Outerspace and the Subsequent Assault of the Equally Evil Lunchroom Zombie Nerds
Captain Underpants and the Perilous Plot of Professor Poopypants

THE HUNDRED AND ONE DALMATIANS • Dodie Smith

The Dearlys' dalmatians deliver a litter of fifteen puppies and everyone is delighted. Cruella de Ville comes home to dinner and the very next day, all the pups go missing. The fur-loving Cruella wants her own fur coat made from the Dalmatian puppies.

Other books by the author:

The Starlight Barking

THE WIND ON THE MOON • Eric Linklater
Major Palfrey is leaving for the wars, and he tells his two girls, Dinah and Dorinda, to be good while he is gone. But the girls are not sure they can be good!

WARRIORS • Erin Hunter
In the Warriors universe there are four clans of wild cats, each with its own unique characteristics. These are the ThunderClan, RiverClan, WindClan and ShadowClan. Fireheart has a pet cat, Rusty, who ventured into the forest to explore the world there and became a member of the ThunderClan. The series follows Fireheart and his adventures,

Other books in the Warrior series:

There are twenty-four books in the series written by Kate Cary, Cherith Baldry and Tui Sutherland under the pseudonym Erin Hunter. The series titles are:

Warriors
Warriors: The New Prophecy
Warriors: Power of Three
Warriors: Omen of the Stars

SIX LIVES OF FANKLE THE CAT • George Mackay Brown
Jenny, a lonely Orkney island girl, gets a skinny black kitten. But Fankle is no ordinary cat. He has lived six lives, all full of adventure and excitement—from ancient Egypt to China, from encountering pirates to winning wars. Jenny does not understand why he would come to Orkney.

TARKA THE OTTER • Henry Williamson
Tarka was a little otter born in a hollow oak by a woodland river.

Deadlock is a pied hound, who is an expert at hunting out the vermin otters. After a nine-hour chase by the pack, Tarka and Deadlock come face to face.

PETER PAN • J.M. Barrie
Peter Pan lives on the island of Neverland and never ages. He lives his never-ending childhood as the leader of the Lost Boys' gang. His best friend is the fairy Tinkerbell.

He visits Kensington Gardens occasionally and he meets Wendy Darling there, and they become close friends.

WILD WOOD • Jan Needle
What if Mr Toad was not really as lovable a character? What if the villains, the Wild Wooders, were not villians at all, but suffering, starving heroes? This is a humorous retelling of *The Wind in the Willows* from the viewpoint of the Wild Wooders where everything the River Bankers did looks like a sham.

RACSO AND THE RATS OF NIMH • Jane Leslie Conly
Rasco makes his way to the Rats colony at Thorn Valley. He does not fit in easily as his father is considered a traitor for deserting the rats and almost causing their extinction. But together with another newcomer, Timothy, Rasco works to sabotage the dam that the humans are building that will submerge the Rats colony.

Other books by the author:
- Mrs Frisby and the Rats of NIMH
- The Silver Crown
- Z for Zachariah
- The Rudest Alien on Earth
- Murder Afloat

While No One Was Watching
Margaret and the Rats of NIMH

JALDI'S FRIENDS • Kalpana Swaminathan
A stray pup, Jaldi, joins the Secret Service of Rani of Bandalbaazi to take on the Mumbai underworld.

THE ADVENTURES OF A NEPALI FROG • Kanak Mani Dixit
A young frog from Kathmandu Valley named Bhaktaprasad Bhyaguto decides to travel his country. He travels through most of Nepal, sharing stories and meeting people, before returning to Kathmandu.

THE TALE OF DESPEREAUX • Kate Dicamillo
'Being the story of a mouse, a princess, some soup, and a spool of thread.' The characters include a very special mouse with an affinity for music, a princess named Pea and Miggery Sow, a poorly-treated, slow-witted serving girl. Since every tale needs a villian, even a sometimes sympathetic one, there is a rat named Roscuro to fill that role.
Other books by the author:
Because of Winn-Dixie
The Tiger Rising
The Magician's Elephant

THE WIND IN THE WILLOWS • Kenneth Grahame
This much-loved story is about Mole, Rat, Toad and Badger who live in the English countryside. Toad is the owner of Toad Hall and is impulsive, brash and always in trouble. Mole, Rat and Badger try and help him improve, but Toad lands up in prison.

ALICE'S ADVENTURES IN WONDERLAND • Lewis Carroll

Join Alice in her adventures as she goes down a rabbit hole, attends a mad tea party, meets the living playing cards and their King and Queen of Hearts.

Other books by the author:
>   Through the Looking-Glass, and What Alice Found There

TIME STOPS FOR NO MOUSE • Michael Hoeye

Hermux Tantamoq, an average mouse, runs a watch shop. Life is normal for him until one day, the daredevil aviatrix Linka comes to his shop to get her watch repaired. Hermux falls in love with her and is plunged into a world of sinister plans and some ruthless rats.

Other books in the Hermux Tantamoq series:
>   The Sands of Time
>   No Time Like Show Time
>   Time to Smell the Roses

Meet the Author
Louis L'Amour

Louis L'Amour was an American author. He wrote novels set in the wild west, which he called Frontier Stories. He also wrote historical fiction, science fiction, non-fiction, poetry and short story collections. He wrote eighty-nine novels, fourteen short story collections and two full-length works of non-fiction.

Some of his series are:
>   The Sackett's Series
>   The Kilkenny Series
>   The Cassidy Novels

TOAD RAGE • Morris Gleitzman

A story about a cane toad named Limpy and his adventures as he tries to save his entire species.

Other books in the Toad series:
- Toad Heaven
- Toad Away
- Toad Surprise

FOUR HEROES AND A HAUNTED HOUSE • Narayan Gangopadhayay

Ths is a translation of a much loved Bengali classic, *Charmurti*. The story is about four friends who go for a holiday and end up at a haunted cottage where ghosts have the weird habit of cackling at night. The four friends are caught up in a series of absurd adventures that include a ferocious Chinese bandit and a sweet-toothed holy man!

THE INCREDIBLE ADVENTURES OF PROFESSOR BRANESTAWM • Norman Hunter

Professor Branestawm is quite mad and terribly absent-minded. He always gets into strange situations, either because of his absent-mindedness or because of the people around him or even his inventions.

Other Professor Branestawm books:
There are thirteen books, some of which are:
- Professor Branestawm Up the Pole
- Professor Branestawm's Perilous Pudding
- Professor Branestawm's Mouse War
- Professor Branestawm's Crunchy Crockery

THE LITTLE BIRD WHO HELD THE SKY UP WITH HIS FEET • Paro Anand

The forest stands still as the black clouds begin to roll in again. Every year, the Monsoon Army's rain comes down harder, destroying trees and plants, nests and burrows. And the rain brings with it gushing, flooded rivers. This year, all the animals know the army will not stop till it has washed away their homes. Should they flee? Should they fight? Or will they trust the unlikeliest hero among them to save their lives?

THE BIG WAVE • Pearl S. Buck

Kino and Jiya live in a fishing village in Japan. A big wave wipes out the whole village, including Jiya's family. As the novel progresses, Jiya rediscovers love, friendship and family.

AWFUL END • Philip Ardagh

Eddie Dickens' parents are sick and he is sent to his Uncle Jack and Aunt Maud's house, Awful End. They turn out to be even more crazy and the book is a hilarious series of adventures told with lots of wordplay.

Other books in the Eddie Dickens trilogy:
Dreadful Acts
Terrible Times

Other books by the author:
The Unlikely Exploits Trilogy

THE CATERPILLAR WHO WENT ON A DIET AND OTHER STORIES • Ranjit Lal

You will see the small creatures of the animal kingdom in a different light after reading this collection of fourteen stories. Meet Nimbu the caterpillar who goes on a diet, Cheeni Chor

the ant who wants the goodies in the refrigerator and Ladoo Gulabjamun, a resident cockroach in the Golden Thali restaurant.
Other books by the author:
> When Banshee Kissed Bimbo and Other Stories
> Small Tigers of Shergarh
> The Life and Times of Altu Faltu
> That Summer at Kalagarh

JUST WILLIAM • Richmal Crompton
William is the leader of the gang of Outlaws and is constantly getting into trouble. There is not a single occasion that almost becomes a disaster thanks to William not thinking through the consequences of his actions.
Other Just William books:
There are a number of Just William books, some of which are:
> More William
> William Again
> William the Fourth
> Still William
> William the Conqueror
> William the Outlaw

AN EPISODE OF SPARROWS • Rumer Godden
A packet of cornflower seeds creates a difference in the lives of slum kids Lovejoy and Tip. They create a garden patch in the disused yard of the Catholic church, but get into trouble for taking mud from the garden in the square.

ASH MISTRY AND THE SAVAGE FORTRESS • Sarwat Chadda
Ash Mistry is forced to come to India, a country he dislikes,

because his uncle has taken up an exciting job with the eccentric Lord Savage. Ash soon gets embroiled in a plan to stop Lord Savage who wants to open the Iron Gates that have kept the demon king Ravana out for nearly four millennia.

Other books by the author:
　Devil's Kiss
　Dark Goddess

THE BOOK OF A THOUSAND DAYS • Shannon Hale

Lady Saren is shut in a tower for seven years for refusing to marry Lord Khasar, who she despises. Her maid Dashti accompanies her and keeps a diary and helps maintain cheer for her mistress.

DOUBLE CLICK! • Subhadra Sen Gupta

Four girls who call themselves the Foxy Four get involved in an adventure when their classmate Simran steps into a mysterious car, gets kidnapped and a ransom note is received. Nothing is as it seems.

Other books in the Foxy Four series:
　Star Struck

Other books by the author:
　Ashoka: The Great and Compassionate King
　Bishnu the Dhobi Singer
　Diary of the World's Worst Cook

YOUNGUNCLE COMES TO TOWN • Vandana Singh

No one knows why Younguncle is called that. The three children are certain of only one thing—when Younguncle comes visiting, there will be adventures and crazy things that will change their lives. And that's what happens!

THE ADVENTURE SERIES • Willard Price

The author wanted to create a series that would be fun and full of adventure that would also get children interested in wildlife and its preservation. Two young zoologists Hal and Roger Hunt take a year's break from school to go around the world and bring back exotic creatures for their father's wildlife collection.

Other books in the series:
- Amazon Adventure
- Whale Adventure
- Gorilla Adventure
- Safari Adventure
- Diving Adventure

WHERE THE RED FERN GROWS • Wilson Rawls

Billy trains his two hunting dogs Dan and Little Ann to hunt raccoons. Billy enters them in raccoon hunting competitions and Dan with his strength and Little Ann with her brains, win the contest. Then a mountain lion changes Billy's life and he has to leave town.

COBRA IN MY KITCHEN • Zai Whitaker

Reptiles like tai-pans and cobras, as well as a few birds and tigers, make an appearance in this collection, set in places such as Papua New Guinea, the Andaman Islands and the Western Ghats.

Other books by the author:
- Andaman Boy

LIONBOY • Zizou Corder

Charlie's scientist parents are kidnapped by an evil pharmaceutical company called Corporacy. Charlie escapes being kidnapped by them and joins a circus ship on its way to Paris. He can understand

and talk the language of cats and befriends six lions who join him in his quest.

Other books in the Lionboy series:

Lionboy: The Chase
Lionboy: The Truth

THE 39 CLUES

Ann and Dan Cahill discover that they belong to a famous family. They must enter a quest and compete with the other branches of the Cahill family to find the 39 clues. These clues are ingredients that will create the most powerful person on Earth.

More in the 39 Clues series:

Series One
The Maze of Bones
One False Note
The Sword Thief
Beyond the Grave
The Black Circle
In Too Deep
The Viper's nest
The Emperor's Code
Storm Warning
Vesper's Rising
Series Two: Cahills vs Vespers
The Medusa Plot
A King's Ransom
The Dead of Night
Shatterproof
Trust No One

LEVEL 2

THE FOUR FEATHERS • A.E.W. Mason
In 1882, Harry Feversham loses the four people he is closest to because he resigns before the expedition to Egypt. His three closest friends present him a white feather each for cowardice. His fiancée gives him a white feather too. Harry is determined to redeem himself and return the feathers.

THE THREE MUSKETEERS • Alexandre Dumas
D'Artagan leaves home and goes to Paris to join the Musketeers of the Guard. His three friends Athos, Porthos and Aramis are the three musketeers and they all live by the motto, 'All for one, one for all'.
Other books in the d'Artagnan romances:
> Twenty Years After
> The Vicomte of Bragelonne: Ten Years Later

THE GUNS OF NAVARONE • Alistair MacLean
A German fortress must be destroyed by an Allied commando team because it is a threat to the Allied naval ships in the Aegean Sea. Two thousand British soldiers are also waiting to be rescued.
Other books by the author:
> HMS Ulysses
> South by Java Head
> The Last Frontier
> Fear is the Key
> The Golden Rendezvous

MINNIE • Annie M.G. Schmidt
Miss Minnie was a cat until she finds herself changed into a

human. While she tries to reverse the change, she befriends a human, Mr Tibbs, when he rescues her from a large dog. She repays him by bringing him information that reveals the truth about one of the town's prominent animal lovers!

THE LITTLE PRINCE • Antoine de Saint-Exupery
A pilot crashes his aircraft and is stranded on a desert when he meets a little boy he calls the little prince. They realize that they understand each other's sketches and drawings that no one else seems to figure out. Over a period of eight days, the pilot and the little prince discuss relationships and life's deeper meanings.
Other books by the author:
Southern Mail
Night Flight
Wind, Sand and Stars

THE KAZIRANGA TRAIL • Arup Kumar Dutta
The Kaziranga National Forest is home to the one-horned rhino. The rhino is endangered and is frequently poached for its horn that is supposed to have medicinal and aphrodisiacal properties. Three local boys find a dead rhino and try to track down the criminals who have done this.
Other books by the author:
The Brahmaputra

CAPTAIN GREY • Avi
Captain Grey is a pirate and takes young Kevin as his prisoner. He wants Kevin to join his group of pirates. But Kevin does not want to. He pretends to obey, but finds out about Grey's past and is determined to escape the ferocious pirate.

Other books by the author:
> The Fighting Ground
> Crispin
> The True Adventures of Charlotte Doyle
> Man from the Sky

AUTUMN OF THE ROYAL TAR • Bruce Stone
A ship called 'Royal Tar' capsizes off the coast of Maine and twelve-year-old Nora's life changes. Between taking care of an elephant and a small boy who are rescued from the ship, Nora's strained relationship with her mother shows signs of improving and Nora comes to terms with the death of her brother a few years ago.

Other books by the author:
> Half Nelson, Full Nelson
> Been Clever Forever

THE POWER OF ONE • Bryce Courtenay
This is the story of an Anglo-African boy who gets nicknamed Peekay. He faces bullying and ragging at school but is gifted in music and trains to become a welterweight boxing champion.

MR MIDSHIPMAN HORNBLOWER • C.S. Forester
Horatio Hornblower starts his career in the Royal Navy as a midshipman, but he is intelligent and smart. He is a good sailor and is a great leader too. He fails sometimes, but those lessons make him better at his work.

Other books in the series:
There are ten books in the series, some of which are:
> Lieutenant Hornblower
> Hornblower and the Hotspur

Hornblower During the Crisis
Hornblower and the Atropos

NO GUNS FOR ASMIR • Christobel Mattingley

A true story of a Bosnian family that escaped war-ravaged Sarajevo. Young Asmir is only seven years old when he escapes with his family. They travel through many countries before becoming refugees in Vienna.

Other books in the series:
Asmir in Vienna
Escape from Sarajevo

INCA GOLD • Clive Cussler

Number twelve in the Dirk Pitt series, *Inca Gold* is about a golden hoard hidden by the ancient Andean people. The golden hoard and the golden chain that holds the key to the hoard remain undiscovered for many years. Now Dirk Pitt and his team get caught up in a plan by an international crime family that wants this treasure and will do anything to get its hands on it.

Other books in the Dirk Pitt series:
There are more than twenty-one books, some of which are:
Sahara
Treasure
Pacific Vortex
Iceberg
Raise the Titanic!

THE THIEF LORD • Cornelia Funke

After escaping their cruel aunt and uncle, orphans Prosper and Bo meet a mysterious boy Scipio who calls himself the 'Thief Lord'. They stay with Scipio's band in an old theatre. Clever and charming, the Thief Lord enjoys making mischief, but he also has a secret.

Other books by the author:
>   Dragonrider
>   Inkheart
>   Reckless

THE HITCHHIKER'S GUIDE TO THE GALAXY • Douglas Adams

Ford Prefect arrives just in time as his friend Arthur Dent is lying in front of the bulldozers. Arthur tries to prevent them from demolishing his house in order to make way for a bypass, not knowing that a larger hyperspace bypass is under construction and the Earth is going to be destroyed. The boys escape in the Vogon's demolition ship and thus begins their journey through the Universe and their misadventures.

Other books in The Hitchhiker's Guide to the Galaxy series:
>   The Restaurant at the End of the Universe
>   Life, the Universe and Everything
>   So Long, and Thanks for All the Fish
>   Mostly Harmless

Other books by the author:
>   Dirk Gently series
>   Last Chance to See
>   The Salmon of Doubt

LASSIE COME HOME • Eric Knight

The journey of a prize collie who braves distances to return to Joe, who she loves.

THE FLIGHT OF THE PHOENIX • Elleston Trevor
A plane crashes in the middle of a desert. The survivors get desperate because the storm has blown them off the course where search teams might be looking for them. One of the survivors claims they can rebuild a new plane from the wreckage of the old. Will the plan work?

BERIC THE BRITON • G.A. Henty
This is the story of a young Briton during the Roman occupation of Britain. He fights the Romans from the swamps and is imprisoned and becomes a gladiator. He kills a lion single-handedly and becomes a guard to the notorious King Nero.

Other books by the author:

G.A. Henty wrote about eighty novels for children, some of which are:

> The Boy Knight: A Tale of the Crusades
> Knight of the White Cross
> With Clive in India: The Beginnings of an Empire
> By Sheer Pluck: A Tale of the Ashanti War

HATCHET • Gary Paulsen
Thirteen-year-old Brian Robeson travels on a Cessna 406 bush plane to visit his father. During the flight, the pilot suffers a heart attack and dies and Brian crash lands the plane into a lake. He has only a hatchet that was a present from his mother, and he manages to survive with the hatchet and his wits for fifty-four days in the wilderness until he is rescued.

Other books in the Hatchet series:

> The River
> Brian's Winter
> Brian's Return

THE TINTIN STORIES • Hergé

A series created by Belgian artist Georges Remi under the pen name of Herge. The series is immensely popular and has been translated into fifty languages and more than two hundred million copies have been sold to date.

The hero of the series is Tintin, a young Belgian reporter who is aided in his adventures by his fox terrier, Snowy. Captain Haddock and Professor Calculus are also popular characters in the series.

Books in the series:

There are twenty-four books in the series, some of which are:

    The Red Sea Sharks
    The Black Island
    The Calculus Affair
    The Castafiore Emerald
    Cigars of the Pharaoh

THE CALL OF THE WILD • Jack London

During the nineteenth century Klondike Gold Rush in the Yukon region, strong sled dogs were in heavy demand. The novel chronicles the experiences of Buck, a domesticated dog who is sold into the brutal life of a sled dog and how he unlearns all his behaviours to become the leader in the wild.

Other books by the author:

    White Fang
    The Sea Wolf

THE ANGEL EXPERIMENT • James Patterson

Six kids who can walk and fly. But something is wrong and these kids are now on the run from the scientists who created them.

Other books in the Maximum Ride series:

    School's Out—Forever

Saving the World and Other Extreme Sports
The Final Warning
Max
Fang
Angel
Nevermore

THE THIRTY-NINE STEPS • John Buchan
In May/June of 1914, Richard Hannay is approached by a spy called Scudder who tells him of a German plot to assassinate the Italian premier and to steal British war plans. Then Scudder is murdered and Hannay decides to carry on the investigation...

Other books featuring Richard Hannay:
Green Mantle
Mr Standfast
The Three Hostages
The Island of Sheep

GULLIVER'S TRAVELS • Jonathan Swift
Lemuel Gulliver loves to travel, a passion which lands him in trouble a number of times. He travels to the land of the Lilliputs, to the land of the giants called Brobdingnag, to a land of deformed savages, Yahoos, and to Laputa, the land where people pursue science without any practical benefits.

THE BAD BEGINNING • Lemony Snickett
The Baudelaire children are doomed...nothing seems to go right for them. They lose their parents in a fire that destroys their house too. They are sent to live with distant relative Count Olaf, who is not the kind of person you might want to live with!

Other books in A Series of Unfortunate Events:
  The Reptile Room
  The Wide Window
  The Miserable Mill
  The Austere Academy
  The Ersatz Elevator

MEET THE AUTHOR
MICHAEL CRICHTON

Michael Crichton was an American author, film producer, film director and television producer. His books sold over 150 million copies worldwide. His works are based on action and feature technology in a big way.

Jurassic Park is a novel about a soon-to-be opened theme park. An astonishing technique for recovering and cloning dinosaur DNA has been discovered. But something goes wrong and science proves to be a dangerous toy.

Some of his other books are:
  Congo
  The Lost World
  The Andromeda Strain
  State of Fear
  Airframe

SMITH: THE STORY OF A PICKPOCKET • Leon Garfield

Smith is a young pickpocket and his life changes when he witnesses a murder. He discovers an important document in the murdered person's belongings and somehow gets blamed for the murder itself.

Other books by the author:
> Black Jack
> Jack Holborn
> The December Rose
> The Apprentices
> John Diamond

MOUSE ATTACK • Manjula Padmanabhan
Arvee is a laboratory rat who becomes a household pet. His new house Paradise Villa is lovely, but there is a devilish Ratlord Pasha, who wants to enslave all the rats with the help of his hench rats. Arvee, with his superior intelligence, has to act. And act smart.

Other books by the author:
> Unprincess!
> Mouse Invaders

THE ADVENTURES OF TOM SAWYER • Mark Twain
Tom Sawyer is a clever little boy who tricks other children into doing his work for him. He turns up at his own funeral and with Huckleberry Finn gets into a series of adventures, including finding a box of gold!

MOONFLEET • Meade J. Falkner
Moonfleet is a small village in the south of England, next to the sea. Legend has it that Colonel Mohune had stolen a diamond from King Charles I. He is buried in the family crypt under the church and his ghost wanders at night in search of the diamond. The mysterious lights in the churchyard are part of his wanderings. Can the orphan John Trenchard unearth the truth?

HOW I LIVE NOW • Meg Rosoff
Fifteen-year-old Daisy is sent from Manhattan to England to visit her aunt and cousins she's never met—three boys near her age, and their little sister. She is happy to escape from her evil stepmother. As war breaks out in London, their lives on the farm change. From food and supplies shortages, to being separated into girl and boy camps, Daisy's fight becomes one of survival.

NEW ARRIVAL AT FOLLYFOOT • Monica Dickens
At Follyfoot Farm, the Colonel looks after old and ill-treated horses, helped by his stepdaughter, Callie, and two stable-hands, Dora and Steve. There is always some adventure and mystery afoot at the farm.

Other books in the Follyfoot series:
> Follyfoot
> Dora at Follyfoot
> The Horses at Follyfoot
> Stranger at Follyfoot

TREASURE ISLAND • R.L. Stevenson
Jim Hawkins finds a mysterious oilskin packet in the belongings of Bones, who dies of a stroke at his parent's inn. It has details of the loot of a pirate Captain Flint and the location of this treasure. A ship sails to find the treasure and on-board is Long John Silver, the very person the dead Bones was wary of meeting. And then there is mutiny on board...

CAPTAIN BLOOD • Rafael Sabatini
Dr Peter Blood does not want to take sides in the fight against the king, but gets convicted. Instead of being hanged, he is sent off to the Caribbean and sold as a slave to work in the sugar plantations.

Other books featuring Captain Blood:
- Captain Blood Returns
- The Fortunes of Captain Blood

Other books by the author:
- The Sea-Hawk
- Scaramouche

PERCY JACKSON AND THE LIGHTNING THIEF • Rick Riordan

Percy Jackson is no ordinary mortal. He is the son of a human and the Greek god Poseidon. He finds himself in Camp Half-Blood with other 'half-bloods' like himself, but is soon sent on a quest when Zeus' lightning bolt has been stolen, and Percy is the prime suspect.

Other books in the Percy Jackson series:
- The Sea of Monsters
- The Titan's Curse
- Percy Jackson and the Sword of Hades
- The Battle of the Labyrinth
- The Last Olympian

THE CORAL ISLAND • Robert M. Ballantyne

Three boys are shipwrecked on a South Pacific island and while they learn to take care of themselves and make the best of what is available to them, they also get into the conflict zone with pirates and Christian converts and non-converts.

Other books by the author:
- The Young Fur-Traders
- The Lighthouse
- The Dog Crusoe

AFTER THE FIRST DEATH • Robert Cormier
A busful of children is hijacked. Every action by the police will result in the death of one of the hijacked children. One of them is the son of a general of an anti-terrorism group.
Other books by the author:
The Chocolate War
I am Cheese
The Rag and Bone Shop

THE JUNGLE BOOK • Rudyard Kipling
The tales in this collection are fables, using animals to give moral lessons. The best known stories in this are those of Mowgli the man-cub, 'Rikki-Tikki-Tavi' and 'Toomai of the Elephants'.
Other books by the author:
Kim
Just So Stories
Captain Courageous
The Man Who Would Be King

THE TRUTH ABOUT FOREVER • Sarah Dessen
Macy suffers the trauma of her father's death. This fear makes her control everything about her life, so she will not face the trauma again. Then Macy meets a bunch of people exactly her opposite and she realizes she had stopped living…

LUWAN OF BRIDA • Sarang Mahajan
Brida is a beautiful small village in the farthest corner of Inkredia, located at the foot of the great Malingo Mountains. But Luwan must escape the village and the dangers for him and his sister there. A perilous journey lies between him and safety.

ISLAND OF THE BLUE DOLPHINS • Scott O'Dell

The story of a young girl stranded for years on an island off the California coast, it is based on the true story of Juana Maria, an Indian left alone for eighteen years on San Nicolas Island in the nineteenth century.

THE AMAZING MAURICE AND HIS EDUCATED RODENTS • Terry Pratchett

The Amazing Maurice runs the perfect Pied Piper scam. He and his 'Educated Rodents' go from town to town pretending to spread the plague. Their accomplice Keith then comes in to rescue the town from the rodents, and they all share the prize money. But conning the town of Bad Blinitz does not go quite as smoothly.

APOCALYPSE • Tim Bowler

Kit and his parents go for a last voyage on their yatch and during a freak accident they get washed up on a hostile island. The community there is hostile and unfriendly. And there are many things that are causing concern here.

RIVER GOD • Wilbur Smith

Taita is a gifted eunuch who joins the Pharoah's service when his master Lord Intef marries off his daughter Lostris to the Pharoah. Lostris loves Tanus, a soldier who incurs the Pharoah's displeasure. Her father also loses favour with the Pharoah. Then the Hykos threaten the Egyptians and Taita must fight with the others to free Egypt.

Other books in the Egyptian series:
> The Seventh Scroll
> Warlock
> The Quest

LEVEL 3

I'D TELL YOU I LOVE YOU, BUT THEN I'D HAVE TO KILL YOU • Ally Carter

Cammie attends The Gallagher Academy that is actually a front for CIA training. Cammie is skilled in languages and trains to kill in many ways, but when she meets Josh, she struggles to keep her secret from him. But Josh is in for a rude shock...

Other books in The Gallagher Girls series:
> Cross My Heart and Hope to Spy
> Don't Judge A Girl by Her Cover
> Only the Good Spy Young
> Out of Sight, Out of Time

THE PRISONER OF ZENDA • Anthony Hope

Rudolf Rassendyll, an Englishman on a holiday in Ruritania, has the strangest experience. The to-be king is drugged on the eve of his coronation and cannot attend the ceremony. But the show must go on, else political machinations threaten the peace and security of the country. Since Rudolf resembles the king, he has to be the body double!

THE LOST WORLD • Arthur Conan Doyle

Malone, a reporter, undertakes a dangerous mission to impress the woman he loves. He manages to get on the right side of Professor Challenger and goes to South America with two other people to see the dinosaurs. A series of challenges later, Malone comes back richer to London only to find that his lady love has married someone else.

THE SCARLET PIMPERNEL • Baroness Orczy

There is a hero who helps aristocrats escape death at the guillotine during the French Revolution. He is a master in disguise and every time he is successful, he leaves a scarlet pimpernel flower to taunt his enemies.

Some other books in the series:
The Elusive Pimpernel
Sir Percy Hits Back
I Will Repay!
The Laughing Cavalier

THE AFRICAN QUEEN • C.S. Forester

Rose wants to avenge her brother's humiliation at the hands of the Germans, and manages to convince Allnutt, the mechanic and skipper of the boat 'African Queen' to help her. They have to make a torpedo that will destroy the German gunboat *Königin Luise*.

THE BIGGLES SERIES • Captain W.E. Johns

James Bigglesworth, aka Biggles, 'loses' his birth certificate and joins the Royal Flying Corps as a scout pilot during World War I. His adventures, and growth from a hysterical teen to a confident competent leader, have made Biggles immensely popular through the decades.

Books in the series:
There are more than ninety Biggles books, some of which are:
The Camels are Coming
The Cruise of the Condor
Biggles of the Camel Squadron
Biggles Flies Again
The Black Peril

CITY OF BONES • Cassandra Clare

Clary sees people that others can't see. She meets Jace, one of the invisible people, and learns that he is a Shadowhunter. Her mother is kidnapped, her apartment trashed and Clary is gravely wounded...

Other books in The Mortal Instruments series:
- City of Ashes
- City of Glass
- City of Fallen Angels
- City of Lost Souls

ROBINSON CRUSOE • Daniel Defoe

Robinson Crusoe does not want to settle down to a boring, predictable life and much against the wishes of his father, decides to go travelling. He becomes a successful plantation owner in Brazil. On a slave gathering expedition to Africa, Crusoe is shipwrecked and spends twenty-seven years on an island.

ANDAMAN: THE JARAWA • Deepak Dalal

Vikram, Aditya and Chitra are three teenagers who go to a forbidden creek in the Andamans to pursue some clues when disaster strikes. They are in the land of the Jarawa, an indigenous people in the lush forests of the Andamans.

Other books by the author:
- Andaman: Barren Island
- Ranthambore Adventure
- Lakshadweep
- Ladakh
- The Snow Leopard

THE TIGERS OF MOMPRACEM • Emilio Salgari
Sandokan and Yanez de Gomera lead the Tigers of Mompracem, a band of rebel pirates fighting against the colonial power of the Dutch and British Empires. Sandokan has become very powerful when he learns of the Pearl of Labuan, a beautiful girl and his fortunes begin to change.

Other books in the series:
> The Pirates of Malaysia
> The Two Tigers

A FAREWELL TO ARMS • Ernest Hemingway
This novel, set during World War I, is a Hemingway classic. Henry, an American, meets Catherine who he falls in love with. Against the backdrop of war, injury and cynicism, their love blossoms, but ends in tragedy.

Other books by the author:
> Old Man and the Sea
> The Sun Also Rises

MASTERMAN READY • Frederick Marryat
The Seagrave family is on a ship en route for Australia. The ship is struck by lightning, the crew escape in the ship's boats and the family is abandoned on board the sinking ship...

Other books by the author:
> The Children of the New Forest

SHE • H. Rider Haggard
Horace Holly journeys with his ward, Leo Vincey, to eastern Africa to look at Leo's mysterious family heritage. They are ship-wrecked and encounter a primitive race of natives and a mysterious white queen who reigns as the all powerful 'She', or

'She-who-must-be-obeyed'.
Other books in the series:
> Ayesha, The Return of the She

Other books by the author:
> The People of the Mist
> King Solomon's Mines
> Cleopatra
> Nada the Lily

PAPILLON • Henri Charrierre
Papillon is a convict who is sent to the penal colony of French Guiana on a wrong charge, from which he decides to escape. Papillon is French for butterfly.

LAST OF THE MOHICANS • James Fenimore Cooper
The story takes place in 1757, during the Seven Years' War, when France and Great Britain battled for control of the North American colonies. The French were supported by their North American allies in this fight. Natty Bumppo is the main hero of the novel.

Other books in the Leatherstocking Tales series:
> The Deerslayer
> The Pathfinder
> The Pioneers
> The Prairie

KANE AND ABEL • Jeffrey Archer
The only common thing between Kane and Abel is their birthday. The men are fiercely ambitious and ruthless and are locked in a relentless struggle.

Other books in the series:
> The Prodigal Daughter

MAN-EATERS OF KUMAON • Jim Corbett

Perhaps the best known of Corbett's books, this contains ten fascinating stories of tracking and shooting man-eaters in the Indian Himalayas during the early years of the last century. Some of the stories in this collection are 'The Chowgarh Tigers', 'The Pipal Pani Tiger' and 'The Kanda Man-eater'.

MEET THE AUTHOR
J.R.R. TOLKEIN

Tolkein was a writer, poet and university professor. He was appointed Commander of the Order of the British Empire by Queen Elizabeth II on 28 March 1972.

He is best known for his classic high fantasy works *The Hobbit*, *The Lord of the Rings* and *The Silmarillion*.

Lord of the Rings refers to the Dark Lord Sauron, who had in an earlier age created One Ring to rule the other Rings of Power, as the ultimate weapon in his campaign to conquer and rule all of Middle-earth. He loses the ring in the battle with the Elves and Men, and wants it back.

SWISS FAMILY ROBINSON • Johann David Wyss

The novel is about the adventures of a Swiss family who weather a great storm and are stranded on a tropical island. Through this book, Wyss wanted to teach his kids about family values, proper usage of natural resources and being self-reliant.

INTO THIN AIR • Jon Krakauer

A true-life account of the author's ascent of Mount Everest in 1996. On May 10 a team began the perilous descent from Mount Everest and eight members were killed in a rogue storm.

TALES FROM THE INDIAN JUNGLES • Kenneth Anderson

Indian-born British Kenneth Anderson was passionate about wildlife. In this collection, his stories are about his adventures in pursuit of man-eating tigers and leopards. The book also gives an insight into the world of the tribal people. Some of the stories in this collection are 'The Aristocrat of Amligola', 'Tales of the Supernatural' and 'The Strange Case of the Gerhetti Leopard'.

Other books by the author:
> The Call of the Man-Eater
> This is the Jungle
> The Black Panther of Sivapalli and Other Adventures of the Indian Jungle
> Nine Man-eaters and One Rogue
> Tiger Roars
> Jungles Long Ago

DAUGHTER OF SMOKE AND BONE • Laini Taylor

Karou lives in Prague, has blue hair and is raised by creatures called the chimaera, who have human and animal features. Karou is with her best friend Zuzana at a restaurant when she receives summons that Brimstone, one of the chimaera, wants her immediately.

Other books in the series:
> Days of Blood and Starlight

MASTER AND COMMANDER • Patrick O'Brian

The first in the naval Aubrey-Maturin series, *Master and Commander* is based on the historical feats of Lord Cochrane in the Napoleonic Wars. Jack Aubrey is the captain of the ship and Stephen Maturin is the ship's surgeon.

Other books in the series:
> There are twenty books in the series, some of which are:
> Post Captain
> HMS Surprise
> The Mauritius Command
> Desolation Island
> The Fortune of War

FACES IN THE WATER • Ranjit Lal
When Gurmeet's mother warns him to not go near the well at their ancestral home, Gurmeet does just that! And he discovers why there are only sons in the Diwanchand family....

Other books by the author:
> The Battle for No. 19
> Bad Moon Rising: Mystery Stories (introduction by the author)
> The Crow Chronicles
> The Life and Times of Altu-Faltu

WATERSHIP DOWN • Richard Adams
Fiver, a runt rabbit, sees a vision that his city is doomed and a group of rabbits leave the city for a new home and a safer future. They are led by Hazel, Fiver's brother, who eventually becomes the Chief Rabbit at the idyllic Watership Down.

STARSHIP TROOPERS • Robert Heinlein
Juan 'Johnnie' Rico is a young soldier from Philippines who enlists in the Mobile Infantry. He becomes an officer in the interstellar war between Bugs and mankind.

TERROR ON THE TITANIC • Samit Basu
Agent Nathaniel Brown of the Morningstar Agency can speak to animals, and has the skills of many jungle creatures. Brown is on the Titanic, to prevent a stolen jewel from returnng to the US. There are some monstrous aliens on the prowl too.

LE MORTE D'ARTHUR • Sir Thomas Malory
This is a compilation of tales of the legendary King Arthur, Guinevere, Lancelot and the Knights of the Round Table. King Arthur became the king of England, won many battles and then consolidated his kingdom. He was advised by Merlin, the wizard.

KON-TIKI • Thor Heyerdahl
Kon-Tiki was the name of the raft Norwegian explorer/author Heyerdahl built and used, documenting his journey in 1947 across the Pacific Ocean from South America to the Polynesian islands.

IVANHOE • Walter Scott
Ivanhoe belonged to one of the remaining Saxon families at a time when the English nobility was predominantly Norman. The book follows the adventures of Ivanhoe who falls out of favour with Cedric, his father, for not only supporting the Norman King Richard I, but also for falling in love with Lady Rowena, who Cedric had planned to marry.

MEET THE AUTHOR
EDGAR RICE BURROUGHS
Burroughs is the creator of the cult figure of Tarzan. He bought a ranch north of Los Angeles, California and named it Tarzana. Today, that little town is called Tarzana in honour of the character.

Though the most popular character he created was Tarzan, Burroughs was a prolific writer and produced a number of science fiction and fantasy series. He was also one of the early writers to recognize the benefits of merchandising his character, and Tarzan appeared in books, movies and comic strips, ensuring his popularity for a long time.

Other books by the author:

Barsroom
Pellucidar
Venus
Caspak
Moon
Mucker

YOUR ADVENTURE CHECKLIST

List the names of the books here as you read them. Rate them and share the ratings with your friends!

Rating scale

Absolutely Smashing—4
Very Good—3
Strictly OK—2
Did Not Like It One Bit—1

Read the Book	Rating

Crime and Mystery

A mysterious death, a robbery, a haunted house, a series of unrelated clues, detectives caught up in resolving the mystery—there's nothing like good mystery stories to get hooked on to reading!

LEVEL 1

PRECIOUS AND THE MYSTERY OF MEERKAT HILL • Alexander McCall Smith
The No. 1 Ladies' Detective Agency series is a very popular mystery series set in Botswana, Africa. They feature Precious Ramotswe as the detective who solves crimes. This one features Precious as an eight-year-old solving her first mysteries.

CHASING VERMEER • Blue Balliett
A letter is delivered to three people with a request to not divulge this to the police. Then, when a Vermeer painting, 'The Lady Writing' gets stolen en route to Chicago's Art Museum, Petra Andalee and Calder Pillay try to piece together the disparate events to locate the painting.
Other books in the Chasing Vermeer series:
>The Wright 3
>The Calder Game

Other books by the author:
Balliet has written a number of books, some of which are:
> The Danger Box
> The Ghost of Nantucket: 23 True Accounts

THE CHAMELEON WORE CHARTREUSE • Bruce Hale

Fourth-grader Chet Gecko has a knack for solving mysteries. His fellow fourth-grader Shirley asks him to find her missing brother Billy and Chet thinks this is going to be easy peasy. The mystery is anything but that…

Other books in the Chet Gecko series:
> The Mystery of Mr Nice
> Farewell, My Lunch Bag
> The Big Nap
> The Hamster of the Baskervilles

THE THIEVES OF OSTIA • Caroline Lawrence

Flavia needs to know why the dogs on her street are dying. She meets a slave Nubia and Jonathan, her new neighbour. When Jonathan's dog is killed and his head taken away, the three friends and Lupus, a mute beggar boy, start the search for the killer.

Other books in the Roman Mysteries series:
> The Secrets of Vesuvius
> The Pirates of Pompeii
> The Assasins of Rome
> The Dolphins of Laurentum

CAM JANSEN AND THE MYSTERY OF THE STOLEN DIAMONDS • David A. Adler

A series of about thirty-five books, the Cam Jansen books are about a fifth-grade female detective named Jennifer 'Cam' Jansen and her best friend Eric. Cam has no supernatural powers except for a photographic memory that comes in handy at solving mysteries.

Some other books in the series:
    Cam Jansen and the Mystery of the Carnival Prize
    Cam Jansen and the Mystery of the Monkey House
    Cam Jansen and the Mystery of the Stolen Corn Popper
    Cam Jansen and the Mystery of Flight 54

Other books by the author:
Adler has written over two hundred books, some of which are:
    The Young Cam Jansen series
    Holocaust Books
    The Bones mystery series
    The Andy Russell series

ENCYCLOPEDIA BROWN • Donald J. Sobol

A series of books featuring the adventures of boy detective Leroy Brown, nicknamed 'Encyclopedia' for his knowledge and intelligence. Brown investigates and cracks petty crimes and solves cases.

Other books in the series:
    Encyclopedia Brown and the Case of the Mysterious Handprints
    Encyclopedia Brown, Boy Detective
    Encyclopedia Brown and the Case of the Secret Pitch
    Encyclopedia Brown Finds the Clues
    Encyclopedia Brown Gets His Man
    Encyclopedia Brown Solves Them All

EMIL AND THE DETECTIVES • Erich Kastner

Emil's first train ride alone and he gets robbed of his precious money when a man drugs him and takes his treasure away. Emil meets Gustav and with twenty-four local children they manage to recover the money.

Other books in the series:
Emil and the Three Twins

SWINDLE • Gordon Korman
After a mean collector named Swindle cons him out of his most valuable Babe Ruth baseball card, Griffin Bing puts into action a plan to recover the card. With a band of misfits, Griffin manages to break into Swindle's high security compound but there is many a hurdle.

Other books in the Swindle series:
Zoobreak
Framed
Showoff
Hideout

POISON ISLAND • H.I. Larry
Twelve-year-old Zac Power comes from a family of spies and no task is too big for him. This time he has to track down an evil mad scientist Dr Drastic, but there is more trouble. Zac's older brother has been kidnapped. He must find Dr Drastic and rescue his brother in time.

Other books in the Zac Powers series:
Deep Waters
Mind Games
Frozen Fear
Sudden Drop

MEET THE AUTHOR
ALEXANDER McCALL SMITH

Smith was born in Bulawayo, present day Zimbabwe. He studied law in Scotland and returned to southern Africa to help set up the framework for a law course, and to teach law at the University of Botswana. He co-wrote the only book on the country's legal system, *The Criminal Law of Botswana*.

Smith is best known for his No. 1 Ladies' Detective Agency series. Precious Ramotswe is the lively intelligent heroine in Botswana who sets up a detective agency 'for all confidential matters and enquiries...under personal management'. She solves cases in her inimitable way.

There are about fourteen books in the series, some of which are:

Tears of the Giraffe
Morality for Beautiful Girls
The Kalahari Typing School for Men
The Full Cupboard of Life

THE SECRET OF THE MANSION • Julie Campbell

Trixie's older brothers are off to a summer camp and she is not too happy about the summer. She must help out with housework and her younger brother. A new girl moves into a neighbouring mansion and an old miser hides a treasure in another one. Then a runaway hides in this mansion.

Other books in the Trixie Belden series:

The Red Trailer Mystery
The Gatehouse Mystery
The Mysterious Visitor
The Mystery off Glen Road

THE DUNDERHEADS • Paul Fleischman
Miss Breakbone is a teacher and hates kids. She gets her just desserts when a bunch of misfits gang up to teach her a lesson.

THE SECRET OF THE TERROR CASTLE • Robert Arthur, Jr.
The Three Investigators, Jupiter, Pete, and Bob want Alfred Hitchhock to use a haunted house in his next movie. Hitchhock agrees, provided they can prove that there is something mysterious going on in the house of former movie star Stephen Terrill, who apparently committed suicide.

Other books in the Three Investigators series:
> The Mystery of the Stuttering Parrot
> The Mystery of the Whispering Mummy
> The Mystery of the Green Ghost
> The Mystery of the Vanishing Treasure

THE BUGALUGS BUM THIEF • Tim Winton
There is a bum thief in Bugalugs and Skeeta, who has also lost his bum sets out to find him.

THE MYSTERIOUS BENEDICT SOCIETY • Trenton Lee Stewart
A mysterious ad appears in the newspaper asking kids if they are gifted and are looking for special opportunities. Loads of children enrol for the tests, but only four special children will be selected to go on a secret mission.

Other books in the Mysterious Benedict Society series:
> The Mysterious Benedict Society and the Perilous Journey
> The Mysterious Benedict Society and the Prisoner's Dilemma

SAMMY KEYES AND THE HOTEL THIEF • Wendelin Van Draanen

Sammy was just killing time when she looked into the hotel across the street with a pair of binoculars. She saw a thief stealing something from one of the rooms, and then invited disaster by waving out to the thief.

Other books in the Sammy Keyes series:
There are seventeen books in the Sammy Keyes series, some of which are:
- Sammy Keyes and the Skeleton Man
- Sammy Keyes and the Sisters of Mercy
- Sammy Keyes and the Runaway Elf
- Sammy Keyes and the Curse of Moustache Mary

LEVEL 2

STORMBREAKER • Anthony Horowitz

Fourteen-year-old Alex Rider suspects that there is more than meets the eye when his uncle is killed. He is told that the uncle died in a car accident, but there are bullet holes in the car's windshield. Alex discovers that his uncle was an undercover spy for MI6 and now he must help look for his assassins.

Other books in the Alex Rider series:
- Point Blanc
- Skeleton Key
- Eagle Strike
- Scorpia
- Ark Angel

Other books by the author:
- The Diamond Brothers series

THE INVENTION OF HUGO CABRET • Brian Selznick

Hugo is an orphan and thief who lives in anonymity and secrecy in a busy Paris train station. But his undercover life is in jeopardy when he attracts the attention of a bookish girl and a bitter old man who runs a toy booth at the station.

BLUE HEAVEN • C.J. Box

Four retired policemen commit a murder and know the two children who have witnessed the event. The children are on the run and can trust no one until they meet Jess, a rancher who will do all he can to protect them.

SILVERFIN: A JAMES BOND ADVENTURE • Charlie Higson

When we first meet young James, he has just started boarding school at Eton in the 1930s. James then teams up with Red, Aflie Kelly's cousin, when Alfie is kidnapped. There is a sinister plot brewing...

Other books in the Young Bond series:
> Blood Fever
> Double or Die
> Hurricane Gold
> By Royal Command

THE GREEN ARCHER • Edgar Wallace

The Green Archer was hanged from a beam at Garre Castle in the fifteenth century and the castle is haunted by his ghost. A Chicago tycoon purchases this castle and imprisons Elaine Held beneath its walls...

Other books by the author:
Wallace wrote more than 175 novels and some of the crime

novels are:
- Angel Esquire
- Terror Keep
- The Crimson Circle
- Kate Plus 10

INSPECTOR GHOTE • H.R.F. Keating

Inspector Ghote belongs to the Bombay C.I.D. and very often finds himself fighting bureaucracy as vigorously as tracking criminals. He is treated with little respect by the rich and powerful but manages to solve cases by his persistence.

Books in the Inspector Ghote series:

There are a number of books featuring the Inspector, some of which are:
- Inspector Ghote's Good Crusade
- Inspector Ghote Caught in Meshes
- Inspector Ghote Hunts the Peacock
- Inspector Ghote Plays a Joker
- Inspector Ghote Breaks an Egg

MEET THE AUTHOR
SIR ARTHUR CONAN DOYLE

Doyle was a Scottish physician and a prolific writer—he wrote science fiction stories, plays, romances, poetry, non-fiction and historical novels.

His best known character is the detective Sherlock Holmes. Using his logical reasoning, his knowledge of forensic science and his ability to disguise himself effectively, Holmes solves cases in the most unusual manner.

In *A Study in Scarlet*, Dr Watson, a military surgeon from the Afghan War needs a flat-mate and Sherlock Holmes needs a foil. He has to solve a peculiar case. There is a corpse, twisted but without wounds facing a deserted house. A mysterious phrase is drawn in blood on the wall and as ever, Scotland Yard is clueless.

Books featuring Sherlock Holmes:

Novels
- The Hound of the Baskervilles
- The Sign of Four
- The Valley of Fear

Short Stories
- The Adventures of Sherlock Holmes
- The Memoirs of Sherlock Holmes
- The Return of Sherlock Holmes
- His Last Bow
- The Case-Book of Sherlock Holmes

ARRIVAL • Michael Teitelbaum

Clark Kent, Lana Lang and Lex Luthor set out on adventures in Smallville in this first book in the series.

Other books in the Smallville series:

There are a number of books in the series, some of which are:
- See No Evil
- Flight
- Animal Rage
- Speed

THE GRACE MYSTERIES • Patricia Finney

Lady Grace Cavendish is a fictional maid of honour to Queen Elizabeth I. This detective series is written in the style of diaries and has Lady Grace solving mysteries.

Books in The Grace Mysteries series:
There are thirteen books in the series, some of which are:
- Assassin
- Betrayal
- Conspiracy
- Deception
- Exile

THE CHERUB SERIES • Robert Muchamore
The British Security Service has a division called CHERUB that employs orphaned minors as intelligence officers. James Adams is part of this division as is his sister Lauren.
There are twelve books in the series, some of which are:
- The Recruit
- Class A
- Maximum Security
- The Killing
- Divine Madness
- Man vs beast

THE RHYTHM OF RIDDLES • Sharadindu Bandhopadhyay
'Truth-seeker' Byomkesh Bakshi and his friend-cum-foil Ajit solve a number of mysteries from a murder to a mystery with a supernatural twist, in this collection of stories.

THE LOCK ARTIST • Steve Hamilton
Michael has not uttered a single word in the last ten years. He can open all kinds of locks and wants to return home to the one person he loves and to unlock the secret that has resulted in his silence for the last ten years.

LEVEL 3

THE MYSTERIOUS AFFAIR AT STYLES • Agatha Christie

When Emily Inglethorp, a wealthy heiress, dies of poisoning, Hercule Poirot tries to piece the evidence together. Her latest will is missing and on the day Emily died, she was overheard arguing with somebody. Is the murderer her much younger husband Alfred or is it her stepson Cavendish?

Books featuring Hercule Poirot:
There are a number of books featuring Poirot, some of which are:
- The Mystery of the Blue Train
- Peril at End House
- Murder on the Orient Express
- Cards on the Table
- Death on the Nile

MURDER AT THE VICARAGE • Agatha Christie

This novel marks the debut of the beloved female detective, Miss Jane Marple. Colonel Protheroe, the magistrate who everyone hates, has been shot through the head. There are many who could potentially be the murderer...

Books featuring Miss Marple:
- 4.50 From Paddington
- The Mirror Crack'd from Side to Side
- Miss Marple's Final Cases and Two Other Stories
- The Moving Finger
- A Murder is Announced

OPEN SEASON • C.J. Box

Joe Pickett is the new game warden in Twelve Sleep, Wyoming, a town where nearly everyone hunts. Unlike his predeccesor the young Joe does not take bribes or look the other way and this causes problems for him.

Other books in the Joe Pickett series:

Savage Run
Winterkill
Trophy Hunt
Out of Range
In Plain Sight

FROM THE MIXED-UP FILES OF MRS BASIL E. FRANKWEILER • E.L. Konigsburg

Claudia Kincaid runs away with her brother and chooses to live in the Metropolitan Museum of Art in the New York City. The children learn to blend with school groups to learn more about the museum, use the pennies in the wish fountain as money for supplies and learn to evade officials who might discover them. They also meet Mrs Basil E. Frankweiler who wants their help.

Other books by the author:

Konigsburg has written many books, some of which are:

The View from Saturday
Silent to the Bone
The Outcasts of 19 Schuyler Place
Father's Arcane Daughter

THE ROMAN HAT MYSTERY • Ellery Queen

During a performance of a play at the Roman Theatre, a lawyer named Monte Field is poisoned. Inspector Richard Queen with his son Ellery investigates the murder. The only clue is that Field's hat is missing...

Books in the Ellery Queen mysteries:

There are many books in the Ellery Queen mysteries, some of

which are:
>   The French Powder Mystery
>   The Dutch Shoe Mystery
>   The Greek Coffin Mystery
>   The Egyptian Cross Mystery
>   The American Gun Mystery

A MORBID TASTE FOR BONES • Ellis Peters

It is 1137 and the head of Shrewsburt Abbey wants the sacred remains of a saint for his Benedictine order. He finds the remains of Saint Winifred in nearby Wales and Brother Cadfael is sent to acquire the sacred remains. While the community debates on whether Cadfael should get possession of the remains, there is a bloody murder.

Other books featuring Brother Cadfael:

There are a number of books in the series, some of which are:
>   One Corpse Too Many
>   Monk's Hood
>   St Peter's Fair
>   The Leper of Saint Giles
>   The Virgin in the Ice

FATHER BROWN • G.K. Chesterton

Father Brown is a character that the author created based on someone he admired. Chesterton met Father O'Connor when he moved from London to Beaconsfield. O'Connor was mild mannered and sharp on the dark behaviours of humans, just like Father Brown.

There are fifty-two short stories that have been compiled into five books:
>   The Innocence of Father Brown

The Wisdom of Father Brown
The Incredulity of Father Brown
The Secret of Father Brown
The Scandal of Father Brown

MEET THE AUTHOR
SATYAJIT RAY

Ray was an Indian film-maker and writer. He was also a publisher, illustrator, graphic designer and film critic.

He created the detective Feluda who is aided by Topshe and the crime-fiction writer Jatayu aka Lalmohan Ganguly. Feluda is strongly built and adept at martial arts, however he relies upon his analytical ability and observation skills to solve cases.

There are a number of books featuring Feluda, some of which are:

The Bandits of Bombay
The Criminals of Kathmandu
The Curse of the Goddess
The Emperor's Ring
The House of Death
Incident on the Kalka Mail
A Killer in Kailash
The Mystery of the Elephant God
The Royal Bengal Mystery
The Secret of the Cemetery

THE SHADOW YEAR • Jeffrey Ford

Strange things happen in what the narrator calls the shadow year. A sixth-grader disappears without a trace, the school librarian goes crazy, the school janitor disappears and is replaced by a stranger and there is a white car that seems to be stalking the narrator.

EVERY SECRET THING • Laura Lippman
Two little girls are banished from a neighbourhood party for a social faux pas, and while on their way home they encounter an abandoned stroller with an infant inside. They are sentenced to seven years in prison for the murder of the infant. And when they are released, babies begin to disappear again...

SHINE • Lauren Myracle
When her best guy friend falls victim to a vicious hate crime, sixteen-year-old Cat sets out to discover who in her small town did it. This novel examines the strength of will it takes to go against everyone you know in the name of justice.

Other books by the author:
>   The Internet Girls series
>   The Winnie Perry series
>   Kissing Kate

MYSTERY MILE • Margery Allingham
Four people have died trying to uncover who may be trying to murder Judge Lobbett. Then the judge disappears. Can Albert Campion solve the mystery in time?

Other Albert Campion books:
There are seventeen novels and over twenty short stories involving Campion, some of which are:
>   Police at the Funeral
>   The Fashion in Shrouds
>   The Tiger in the Smoke
>   The Case of the Late Pig
>   The Border-Line Case

THE CURIOUS INCIDENT OF THE DOG IN THE NIGHT-TIME • Mark Haddon

Fifteen-year-old Christopher Boone has issues. He is autistic, relaxes by solving math problems in his head and eats red, but not yellow or brown foods. His neighbour's poodle is murdered and Christopher decides to find the killer and unearths dark secrets!

DEATH IN KASHMIR • M.M. Kaye

Sarah Parrish takes a skiing vacation to Gulmarg in Kashmir. Her idyllic holiday is disturbed when two members of her team are murdered. She is entrusted with a mission. Will she achieve what she has to and be with her newly found love?

Other books in the Death in series:
- Death in the Andamans
- Death in Berlin
- Death in Cyprus
- Death in Zanzibar

HAWKSMOOR • Peter Ackroyd

Detective Hawksmoor investigates the gruesome murders on the sites of some eighteenth-century churches. He unwittingly forms an alliance with the very devil he is seeking—Nicholas Dyer, who lived two hundred and fifty years ago and concealed a dark secret in each of the seven churches he was commissioned to build.

Other books by the author:
- Chatterton
- The Last Testament of Oscar Wilde
- The House of Dr Dee

THE BIG SLEEP • Raymond Chandler

Philip Marlowe is entrusted with handling the blackmailer of a millionaire's troublesome daughter and finds that there is more than meets the eye. The blackmailer has been shot dead, a gangster confronts Marlowe about the death of the blackmailer, and the other daughter's husband Rusty is also missing.

Other books in the Philip Marlowe series:

　Trouble is My Business
　Farewell, My Lovely
　The High Window
　The Lady in the Lake
　The Little Sister
　The Simple Art of Murder
　The Long Goodbye
　Playback

FER-DE-LANCE • Rex Stout

Archie Goodwin is investigating the apparently disconnected murders of an immigrant and a college president. Then he receives a gift of a Fer-de-Lance, one of the deadliest snakes and Goodwin realizes he is close to solving the murders.

Books in the Nero Wolfe series:

There are a number of books in the Nero Wolfe series, some of which are:

　The League of Frightened Men
　The Rubber Band
　The Red Box
　Too Many Cooks

THE DEVIL YOU KNOW • Wayne Johnson

Max is an alchoholic who returns to his family and plans a canoe trip with his kids. The idyllic trip turns into a nightmare when rednecks from a meatpacking plant in the vicinity murder their supervisor and in the angry haze come after Max and his family.

MEET THE AUTHOR
THE STRATEMEYER SYNDICATE

Created by Edward Stratemeyer, the Stratemeyer Syndicate was the first book packager to have its books aimed at children. Edward Stratmeyer aimed to produce books in an efficient assembly-line fashion and to write them in such a way as to maximise their popularity.

The Nancy Drew and Hardy Boys series produced by the syndicate are the best known. There were some guidelines that were followed for the books:

- The first several volumes of a new series would be published at once. These 'breeders' would establish the series successfully.
- The books would be written under a pseudonym, so that other ghost writers could also write books.
- The books would look like adult novels.
- Chapters and pages would end mid-situation to increase the reader's desire to keep reading!

Some of the titles are:

Nancy Drew Series, Carolyn Keene
Nancy Drew Mystery Story Series 1: fifty-six books
Nancy Drew Mystery Story Series 2: 132 books
Nancy Drew Files: 124 books
Nancy Drew on Campus: twenty-five books
Nancy Drew Girl Detective: twelve books till date
The Nancy Drew Notebooks: sixty-five books
The Nancy Drew Graphic Novels: three till date

Hardy Boys Series, Franklin W Dixon
Hardy Boys Mystery Stories Series 1: fifty-eight books
Hardy Boys Mystery Stories Series 2: 132 books
The Hardy Boys Casefiles: 127 books
The Hardy Boys: The Clues Brothers: seventeen books till date
The Hardy Boys: Undercover Brothers: seven books till date
The Hardy Boys Graphic Novels: three books till date
The Nancy Drew and Hardy Boys Supermysteries

YOUR CRIME FICTION CHECKLIST

List down the books as you read them. Also rate them and share the ratings with your friends!

Rating scale

    Absolutely Smashing—4
    Very Good—3
    Strictly OK—2
    Did Not Like It One Bit—1

Read the Book	Rating

Fantasy

Magic and wizards, vampires and otherworldly beings—fantasy novels make us travel to other worlds. Try these ones listed here!

LEVEL 1

THE WEIRDSTONE OF BRISINGAMEN • Alan Garner

The weirdstone of Brisingamen was lost centuries ago and now, a young girl Susan wears it in her silver bracelet. When she and her brother Colin realize the importance of the white magic stone, they set out to find the custodian, the wizard Cadellin.

Other books in the series:

The Moon of Gomrath

WORZEL GUMMIDGE: THE SCARECROW OF SCATTERBROOK FARM • Barbara Euphan Todd

Gummidge is a scarecrow who is supposed to defend the Scatterbrook Farm from crows. He has a set of interchangeable heads that give him a specific skill. But Gummidge is more interested in Aunt Sally, a fairground doll, and his friends John and Susan have to bail him out of the sticky situations he gets into.

Other books in the Worzel Gummidge series:

Worzel Gummidge Again

More About Worzel Gummidge

Worzel Gummidge and Saucy Nancy
Worzel Gummidge Takes a Holiday
Earthy Mangold and Worzel Gummidge

REDWALL • Brian Jacques

The series is set in the world of Redwall that has a bit of magic and animals that can talk. Martin the Warrior often appears in dreams or hallucinations giving valuable information in the form of a riddle that must be solved.

Books in the Redwall series:

There are many books in the series, some of which are:
Mossflower
Mattimeo
Mariel of Redwall
Salamandastron

STIG OF THE DUMP • Clive King

Stig is Barney's secret friend. He is a caveman and lives at the bottom of the old quarry where people dump all kinds of stuff. Together the two have loads of adventures, and then one day, they are transported back in time to Stig's era.

Other books by the author:

Me and My Million
The Town that Went South
The Twenty-Two Letters
The Night the Water Came

HOWL'S MOVING CASTLE • Diana Wynne Jones

Sophie lived in the town of Market Chipping in the magical kingdom of Ingary. She is the eldest in the family and local lore has it that the eldest child can never be successful. But Sophie is

deft with the needle and can talk life into inanimate objects. Then, she is turned into an old woman by the Witch of the Waste...
Other books in the Howl's Moving Castle series:
  Castle in the Air
  House of Many Ways

IN SEARCH OF WATER • Dilip M. Salwi
An alien arrives on Earth in search for pure water. Young Tina sets out to help him, but discovers it is next to impossible to get even a drop of pure water on Earth. What is going on?

SO YOU WANT TO BE A WIZARD • Diane Duane
Nita discovers a book that claims that if she takes the Wizard Oath, she can become a wizard. Not really believing the book, she takes the oath and soon realizes that she is indeed a wizard now!
Other books in the Young Wizards series:
There are ten books in the series, some of which are:
  Deep Wizardry
  High Wizardry
  A Wizard Abroad
  The Wizard's Dilemma

THE WONDERFUL FLIGHT TO THE MUSHROOM PLANET • Eleanor Cameron
Mr Bass is a funny-looking scientist and he sends a spaceship with two boys to the planet of Basidium that is house to the Mushroom people. The people there are dying because of a mysterious illness and the boys must find a solution, along with their mascot, a hen.

THE ENCHANTED WOOD • Enid Blyton
Jo, Bessie and Fanny move to the country and find an Enchanted

Wood right on their doorstep! And in the woods stands the magic Faraway Tree that can transport them to different worlds. The children must remember to come back before the lands move, else they can be stuck there forever.

Other books in the series:
The Magic Faraway Tree
The Folk of the Faraway Tree
Up the Faraway Tree

THE WONDERFUL WIZARD OF OZ • Frank Baum

In a hurricane, Dorothy and her dog are swept away to the Land of Oz. She wants to come back home and goes down the Yellow Brick Road to find the wizard who can send her back home. On the way, she meets the Scarecrow without brains, the Tinman without a heart and a Lion who lacks courage…

GLUBBSLYME • Jacqueline Wilson

Rebecca Brown gets into a fight with her best friend Sarah who goes off with Mandy. Rebecca meets Glubbslyme, not an ordinary toad. And they get into many adventures.

MEET THE AUTHOR
EVA IBBOTSON

Eva was an Austrian born, British novelist. Her books are imaginative and humorous, and most feature magical creatures and places. *Journey to the River Sea* was written in honour of her husband, who was a naturalist. She loved nature and that is evident in many of her books.

In *The Secret of Platform 13*, a forgotten door on an abandoned railway platform is the entrance to a magical kingdom. This is an island that is hidden from the world and is accessible only when a secret door opens for nine days once every nine years.

Ibbotson has written many books, some of which are:
- A Countess Below Stairs
- A Company of Swans
- Which Witch
- Island of the Aunts

MIDNIGHT FOR CHARLIE BONE • Jenny Nimmo

Charlie can hear people talking and thinking in photographs. He is no ordinary boy, but the descendant of the Red King. Now he has to attend the Bloors Academy for gifted children.

Other books in the Charlie Bone series:
- Charlie Bone and the Time Twister
- Charlie Bone and the Blue Boa
- Charlie Bone and the Castle of Mirrors
- Charlie Bone and the Hidden King

THE PHANTOM TOLL BOOTH • Juster Norton

Milo is bored. When a toll booth appears in his room, Milo drives through it into the Kingdom of Wisdom where everything is unexpected and many characters abound.

Other books by the author:
- The Hello, Goodbye Window
- Neville
- The Odious Ogre
- Sourpuss and Sweetie Pie
- Alberic the Wise

BRIDGE TO TERABITHIA • Katherine Paterson

Jess Aaron gets outrun by Leslie on the first day of school but they soon become inseparable. The children create a magical kingdom called Terabithia in the neighboring woods, where they reign as king and queen.

THE BOOK OF THREE • Lloyd Alexander

Taran the Assistant Pig Keeper wants to become a hero. His pig, who can tell the future runs away and Taran plunges deep into the woods to find him. He finds many other characters and becomes involved in the epic struggle of good and evil .

Other books in The Chronicles of Prydain series:
- The Black Cauldron
- The Castle of Llyr
- Taran Wanderer
- The High King

Other books by the author:
- The Westmark series
- Time Cat

INDIAN IN THE CUPBOARD • Lynne Reid Banks

Ohri is unimpressed with the little plastic toy he receives on his birthday. But when he puts that toy in his cupboard, the Indian comes to life who can be quite demanding.

Other books in The Indian in the Cupboard series:
- The Return of the Indian
- The Secret of the Indian
- The Mystery of the Cupboard
- The Key to the Indian

THE BORROWERS • Mary Norton

The Borrowers are the tiny Clock family who live beneath the kitchen floor of an old manor. They 'borrow' their possessions from the human 'beans' on the top. All goes well, till a human boy spots one of them.

Other books in The Borrowers series:

The Borrowers Afield
The Borrowers Afloat
The Borrowers Aloft
The Borrowers Avenged

CORALINE • Neil Gaiman

Coraline moves into a new home with her parents. She discovers a brick wall behind a door and that leads her into a magical world. Coraline comes back from this weird world where she has another set of parents to find that her real parents have disappeared.

Other books by the author:

The Sandman series
Good Omens
Fortunately the Milk

TUCK EVERLASTING • Natalie Babbitt

Winnie Foster wants to explore the world, but she is only ten years old. She meets the Tuck family who are blessed with eternal life and they teach her about life and the meaning of love and friendship.

THE ENORMOUS EGG • Oliver Butterworth

A hen lays an enormous egg on Nate's family farm and a little triceratop is born. Nate names it Beazley, but he has no idea what to expect when you make a dinosaur your pet.

Other books by the author:

The Trouble with Jenny's Ear
The Narrow Passage

THE AKHENATEN ADVENTURE • P.B. Kerr
Twelve-year-old twins John and Philippa Gaunt discover that like their mother and Uncle Nimrod, they are djinns. They have extraordinary powers and embark on an adventure to locate the Egyptian pharaoh Akhenaten and his eerie tomb.
Other books in the Children of the Lamp series:
> The Blue Djinn of Babylon
> The Cobra King of Kathmandu
> The Day of the Djinn Warriors
> The Eye of the Forest

MARY POPPINS • P.L. Travers
Mary Poppins arrives as a governess at Number Seventeen Cherry Tree Lane and the lives of the Bank family are changed forever. With her sensible hat and parrot umbrella, Mary sets about disciplining the children with a bit of magic and common sense.
Other Mary Poppins books:
There are a number of Mary Poppins books, some of which are:
> Mary Poppins Comes Back
> Mary Poppins Opens the Door
> Mary Poppins in the Park
> Mary Poppins in the Kitchen

BEAUTY • Robin McKinley
A beloved retelling of the tale of the fairytale 'Beauty and the Beast' showing how true love surpasses all.
Other books by the author:
> The Hero and the Crown
> Deerskin
> Sunshine

PRINCESS ACADEMY • Shannon Hale
Miri lives on Mount Eskel where her ancestors have quarried stone for generations. Word comes that the king's priests have forseen that the future princess will come from this community. A princess academy is set up and Miri excels there. Who will she marry? The handsome prince or her friend Peder?

Other books by the author:
> Book of a Thousand Days
> Goose Girl

ADITI AND THE ONE-EYED MONKEY • Suniti Namjoshi
A monkey, an elephant and an ant set out to explore the world En route they meet Princess Aditi and decide to help this girl with a mission.

There are more books in the Aditi series, some of which are:
> Aditi and the Thames Dragon
> Aditi and the Marine Sage
> Aditi and the Techno Sage

THE MOOMINS AND THE GREAT FLOOD • Tove Janesson
The Moomins, creatures always ready for adventure, find a magical hat. Moominmamma and Moomintroll search for Moominpappa who was lost at sea with the magical hat that can turn into anyone and anything.

Other books in The Moomin series:
> There are many books in the series, some of which are:
> Comet in Moominland
> Finn Family Moomintroll
> Moominpappa's Memoirs
> Moominsummer Madness

THE PRINCESS BRIDE • William Goldman

A handsome young farmhand Westley finds his love reciprocated by the beautiful Buttercup. He leaves to seek a fortune and is believed to be killed by the dreaded pirates. Meanwhile, Buttercup agrees to marry Prince Humperdinck , but is kidnapped.

LEVEL 2

EVERYBODY SEES THE ANTS • A.S. King

Lucky Linderman is not very lucky...he has a dysfunctional family and is the target of Nader the bully. After a bullying episode that is horrifying, he begins to see ants who act like a chorus and express his thoughts and feelings.

Other books by the author:
- Please Ignore Vera Dietz
- The Dust of 100 Dogs
- Ask the Passengers

BEASTLY • Alex Flinn

A story from the perspective of the Beast in the 'Beauty and the Beast'. Kyle is a popular, attractive kid who gets turned into a beast when he plays a prank on the wrong person. He has two years to find a girl who will love him and who he will love too if he is ever to get back to his human form again.

THE PELLINOR • Alison Croggon

A fantasy series, Pellinor features Maerad, a slave who lives in the world of Edil-Amarandh. She has a Gift and is able to command the nature at her will. Is she the Foretold One who will defeat the corruption in the land and The Nameless One?

Books in the series:
- The Gift
- The Riddle
- The Crow
- The Singing

MAGYK • Angie Sage

Silas Heap discovers an unusual baby with violet eyes in the snow and takes her home to raise as his home. His own son Septimus died on birth and the little infant Jenna's origins have to be kept a secret. But is Septimus really dead?

Other books in the Septimus Heap series:
- Flyte
- Physik
- Queste
- Syren
- Darke

FABLEHAVEN • Brandon Mull

Kendra and Seth spend time with their grandparents while their parents are off on a cruise. Grandpa is missing and Grandmother gives them a puzzle to solve. Once the children decipher the puzzle they drink the milk set out in the yard for them every morning. They are transported to the mystical, magical world of Fablehaven that is not as idyllic as it looks where they meet Grandpa.

Other books in the Fablehaven series:
- Rise of the Evening Star
- Grip of the Shadow Plague
- Secrets of the Dragon Sanctuary
- Keys to the Dragon Prison

WHATEVER BECAME OF THE SQUISHIES • Claire Chilton

Carla is a misfit and trouble follows her everywhere. She is a purple person, an outcast, living in a colony of green. Should she be inheriting special powers?

Other books in the Whatever Became of the Squishies series:
- Shattered

INKHEART • Cornelia Funke

Mo, the father of twelve-year-old Meggie, can 'read' fictional characters to life. One of these is the unhappy Dustfinger who misses his troll and fairy friends, and Capricorn, a character so evil that his heart is made of ink. Capricorn wants Mo's skill—for evil of course.

Other books in the series:
- Inkspell
- Inkdeath

Other books by the author:
- The Reckless Series
- The Ghosthunter Series
- The Thief Lord
- Dragon Rider
- When Santa Fell to Earth
- Igraine the Brave
- Saving Mississippi
- Ghost Knight

JACKAROO • Cynthia Voigt

Things are not right in the kingdom and there is talk of Jackaroo, the legend who helps the poor. Gwyn does not believe in these

tales but one day, stranded in a snowstorm, Gwyn discovers something that convinces her that Jackaroo is not a myth.
Other books in The Kingdom series:
   On Fortune's Wheel
   The Wings of a Falcon
   Elske

SKELLIG • David Almond
Michael's life is not going too well. His little infant sister is born with a damaged heart and may not live. In the new garage, Michael encounters a dirty tramp who eats spiders and mice. But an act of kindness changes Michael's world forever.
Other books by the author:
   Kit's Wilderness
   My Name is Mina
   Heaven Eyes
   Clay

ARTEMIS FOWL • Eoin Colfer
Captain Holly Short of LEPrecon has exhausted her magical abilities while on duty. She is on her way to Ireland for a ritual to rejuvenate herself when she is kidnapped by Artemis Fowl who is an arch criminal. He wants some of the Hostage Fund to support his dwindling funds.
Books in the Artemis Fowl series:
   Artemis Fowl: The Arctic Incident
   Artemis Fowl: The Seventh Dwarf
   Artemis Fowl: The Eternity Code
   Artemis Fowl: The Opal Deception
   Artemis Fowl: The Lost Colony
   Artemis Fowl: The Time Paradox

Other books by the author:
> The Supernaturalist
> Airman
> The Wishlist

SABRIEL • Garth Nix
Sabriel is an Abhorsen, those beings who can pass from the land of the living to that of the dead. When her father, an Abhorsen whose job it is to protect the living from the dead, goes missing, Sabriel must enter the Old Kingdom to find him.

Other books in the Abhorsen trilogy:
> Lirael
> Abhorsen

ENTWINED • Heather Dixon
A take on the fairy tale of the 'Twelve Dancing Pricesses'. To escape the sadness and grief of their mother's death, Azalea and her sisters dance in the mysterious silver forest each night. Azalea trusts the handsome Keeper, and then begins to realize that he is upto no good.

TITHE: A MODERN FAERIE TALE • Holly Black
Sixteen-year-old Kaye Fierch tours the country with her mother's rock band. After her mother's boyfriend attempts to stab her mother, the two return to their hometown. Kaye becomes aware that she is a faery and gets drawn into a fight between Faery factions.

Other books in Modern Faerie Tales:
> Valiant
> Ironside

THE SPIDERWICK CHRONICLES • Holly Black and Tony DiTerlizzi

The Grace children, twins Simon and Jared, and Malory move into the Spiderwick Estate and discover their great uncle's Field Guide. It leads them to a magical world of faeries that include fantastical creatures like brownies and elves. Everyone in that world wants the Field Guide!

Books in the Spiderwick Chronicles series:
- The Spiderwick Chronicles: The Field Guide
- The Spiderwick Chronicles: The Seeing Stone
- The Spiderwick Chronicles: Lucinda's Secret
- The Spiderwick Chronicles: The Ironwood Tree
- The Spiderwick Chronicles: The Wrath of Mulgarath

THE AMULET OF SAMARKAND • Jonathan Stroud

Nathaliel is a magician's young apprentice who does not think too much of his skill. But the apprentice has been reading his master's books and summons the 5,000-year-old-djinni Bartimaeus who does not want to do his bidding. Nathaliel is locked in two struggles—to gain power over Bartimaeus and to avenge his humiliation at the hands of Simon Lovelace. But Lovelace is more evil than the young boy fathoms.

Other books in the Bartimaeus Trilogy:
- The Golem's Eye
- Ptolemy's Gate

Other books by the author:
- Heroes of the Valley
- Buried Fire
- The Leap
- The Last Siege

MEET THE AUTHOR
C.S. LEWIS

Known to his family and friends as Jack, C.S. Lewis was a novelist, poet and academic. He served on the English faculty at Oxford University and was active in the informal Oxford literary group known as the 'Inklings'.

Lewis is well known for both his fictional and non-fictional works, the best known being the seven-book series *The Chronicles of Narnia*. Set in the fictional world of Narnia, the series narrates the adventures of various children who play key roles in its unfolding history.

Books in the series:
- The Lion, the Witch and the Wardrobe
- The Magician's Nephew
- The Horse and His Boy
- Prince Caspian
- The Voyage of the Dawn Treader
- The Silver Chair
- The Last Battle

HANNAH • Kathryn Lasky

Hannah spent her early days in an orphanage and is now a scullery maid in the house of a rich, powerful family. She is affected by the ocean and feels sick when she is away from it, shedding salt crystals and longing to be in water. Is she more than just a poor scullery maid?

THE SUMMONING • Kelley Armstrong

Chloe starts seeing ghosts and is locked up in a home for unstable children. Among her new friends are a werewolf, a half demon and a witch spell-caster.

Other books in The Darkest Powers series:
- The Awakening
- The Reckoning

A GREAT AND TERRIBLE BEAUTY • Libba Bray
After the tragic death of her mother, Gemma goes to a boarding school in England where she befriends three girls. They discover a secret magical world called the realms...but there are some who want to use the magic there for their own purposes.
Other books in The Gemma trilogy:
- Rebel Angels
- The Sweet, Far Thing

CITY OF MASKS • Mary Hoffman
Lucien is seriously ill but he becomes a stravagante, a time traveller to sixteenth-century Italy. There he meets Arianna and becomes a mandolier.
Other books in the Stravaganza series:
- City of Stars
- City of Flowers
- City of Secrets
- City of Ships
- City of Swords

SHADOW CHILDREN • Margaret Peterson Haddix
Luke is a shadow child—the third child forbidden by the Population Police. He has never had a friend, never been to a party and has always lived his life in hiding. He meets another shadow child, and his life changes.
Other books in the Shadow Children series:
- Among the Imposters

Among the Betrayed
Among the Barons
Among the Brave
Among the Enemy
Among the Free

THE PRINCESS DIARIES • Meg Cabot

Fourteen-year-old Mia Thermopolis is a regular teenager in New York City. She discovers that she is the heiress to the throne of Genovia. The world changes when she becomes a princess...

Other books in The Princess Diaries series:
Princess in the Spotlight
Princess in Love

Other books by the author:
Queen of Babble series
The Mediator series
Heather Wells series
All American Girl series

A SPELL FOR CHAMELEON • Piers Anthony

Bink is a misfit in the magical land of Xanth. Everyone there has a magical talent. Bink must find his magical talent, else he will lose his home and his fiancée.

Other books in the Xanth series:
The Source of Magic
Castle Roogna
Ogre Ogre
Night Mare

KEEPER MARTIN'S TALES: THE KINGDOM AND THE ELVES OF THE REACHES • Robert Stanek

Ruin Mist was a place where magic abounded till the great kings

decreed that magic would be cleansed to dust. The only hope is the elf Queen Mother who can lead them from darkness.
Other books in the series:
> The Kingdom and the Elves of the Reaches 2
> The Kingdom and the Elves of the Reaches 3
> The Kingdom and the Elves of the Reaches 4
> In the Service of Dragons
> In the Service of Dragons 2

Other books by the author:
> Ruin Mist Tales

TARANAUTS: THE QUEST FOR THE SHYN EMERALDS • Roopa Pai

Shyn, Dazl, Glo, Shimr, Lustr, Sparkl, Syntilla, Glytr… These are the bright, shining worlds of a whole different universe called Mithya. But now all eight are in darkness. Mithya's thirty-two stars have been seized by Shaap Azur. Three brave and gifted Taranauts—Zarpa, Zvala and Tufan—come to their rescue.
There are seven books in the series. Some of them are:
> The Riddle of the Lustr Sapphires
> The Secret of the Sparkl Amethysts
> The Race for the Glo Rubies
> The Mystery of the Syntilla Silvers

DOA DETECTIVE FILES: TROUBLE AT THE TAJ • Sonja Chandrachud

Natural or supernatural, no mystery is out of this world for the Dead or Alive Detective Agency. Travel back in time to when the Taj Mahal is under construction with the DOA gang as they solve out-of-this-world mysteries using their wits, will and Tuk Tuk, their auto rickshaw with attitude, which also happens to

be a time machine!
Other books by the author:
> DOA Detective File: Revenge of the Pharaoh
> The Hilarious Hauntings series

THE CRY OF THE ICEMARK • Stuart Hill

The Icemark is a kingdom in grave danger with its king dead and the enemy waiting to attack. The princess Thirrin finds a companion in Oskan Witch and together they must save the kingdom.

Other books in the series:
> Blade of Fire
> Last Battle of the Icemark

OVER SEA, UNDER STONE • Susan Cooper

On holiday in Cornwall, the three Drew children discover an ancient map in the attic of the house they are staying in. It seems to belong to the time of King Arthur and is the key to finding the Grail but soon the agents of the Dark are out to get them.

Other books in The Dark is Rising series:
> The Dark is Rising
> Greenwitch
> The Grey King
> Silver on the Tree

ALANNA: THE FIRST ADVENTURE • Tamora Pierce

Alanna wants to be a knight and go on missions and adventures that are reserved only for the boys. Her brother wants to learn magic. So the two kids switch places and Alanna heads to the king's castle to become a page.

Other books in The Song of The Lioness quartet:
- In the Hand of the Goddess
- The Woman Who Rides like a Man
- Lioness Rampant

Other books by the author:
- The Immortals series
- Emelan series
- Protector of the Small series

THE SWORD OF SHANNARA • Terry Brooks

In the world of the Four Locks, Shea must find the Sword of Shannara and stop the evil Warlock Lord. Prince Balinor must also dethrone his crazy brother and protect the kingdom of Callahorn from the Warlock Lord.

THE MAGICIAN'S GUILD • Trudi Canavan

Sonea is a slum girl who possesses magical abilities generally restricted to the upper classes. She tries to escape the Magician's Guild who she thinks is out to get her...

Books in the Black Magician series:
- The Novice
- The High Lord
- Prequel: The Magician's Apprentice
- Sequel: The Traitor Spy trilogy

Other books by the author:
- Millennium's Rule series
- The Traitor Spy series
- The Age of the Five

SWORDS FOR HIRE: TWO OF THE MOST UNLIKELY HEROES YOU'LL EVER MEET • Will Allen

The country of Parmall is in distress. The rightful king has been imprisoned and the usurper wants to marry the beautiful damsel in distress. All hope rests on Sam Hatcher and Rigby Skeet.

LEVEL 3

EVERMORE • Alyson Noel

Sixteen-year-old Ever Bloom can see people's auras, hear their thoughts and know their life story simply by touching them. She is considered a freak in her school and then she meets Damen Auguste who intrigues her because she cannot read his aura.

Other books in The Immortals series:
Eternal Flame
Blue Moon
Shadowland
Dark Flame
Night Star
Everlasting

BLOOD AND CHOCOLATE • Annette Curtis Klause

Vivian is a Homo lupus and enjoys her ability to change from girl to wolf. She has many a wolf admirer, but she likes the human Aiden. Can she let him into her secret?

Other books by the author:
The Silver Kiss
Alien Secrets
Freaks: Alive, on the Inside!

INCARCERON • Catherine Fisher
Incarceron is a massive futuristic jungle complete with cells, dilapidated cities and towers. Finn lives there but believes there is a world outside Incareron. He chances upon a crystal key and establishes contact with Claudia, the daughter of the Warden, who claims she lives on the Outside.

Other books in the Incarceron series:
- Sapphique

THE INHERITANCE CYCLE • Christopher Paolini
In the fictional world of Alagaesia, Eragon and his dragon Saphira, along with his cousin Rorin and Nasuada, the leader of the Vardin, fight to stop the evil Galbatorix from conquering the world.

Books in The Inheritance Cycle series:
- Eragon
- Eldest
- Brisingr
- Inheritance

THE MAGIC CIRCLE • Donna Jo Napoli
What is the true story of the witch in the Hansel and Gretel stories? Well, she was actually a mid-wife who turned a healer and had the ability to keep the demons at bay. She was tricked and became a witch.

TIGANA • Guy Gavriel Kay
Tigana was once a beautiful land. But the brutally oppressed people, who have lost their books, architecture and everything else are forbidden to ever speak the name of their homeland or to even dare to remember it.

THE WORDKEEPERS • Jash Sen
It is 2028. Anya is an average spoilt teenager, living in Bangalore. Bilaal is a carefree village boy, in rural Andhra Pradesh. Their ordinary, humdrum lives hide an ancient secret, which will turn their worlds upside down and throw them into a terrifying adventure whose outcome can affect, not just their lives, but the fate of the entire universe.

Other books in the trilogy:
Skyserpents

VIMANA • Mainak Dhar
We think the myths and legends are just that. But a young college student realizes that the gods have returned to fight the war that was started fifteen thousand years ago. And the myths are actually true.

Other books by the author:
Alice in Deadland
Zombiestan

MEET THE AUTHOR
SIR TERRY PRATCHETT

Pratchett is an English author of fantasy novels, best known for the Discworld series of about forty volumes. Since 1983, when he wrote the first *Discworld* novel, he wrote two books a year on average. He has sold over seventy million books in thirty-seven languages.

Pratchett loves wearing large, black fedora hats! He loves astronomy and has an observatory in his garden. An asteroid, 127005 Pratchett, is named after him.

In the book *Truckers*, part of the Bromeliad Trilogy, there is a world of the gnomes under the Store that humans are unaware of. Then one day, a group of gnomes arrives on a truck, talking crazy legends like Day and Night and the devastating news that the Store is to be demolished.

Other books in the Bromeliad Trilogy:
  Diggers
  Wings

Other books by the author:
  The Johnny Maxwell Series
  The Discworld Series
  Accurate Prophecies of Agnes Nutter, Witch

LEGEND • Marie Lu

The novel is set in the ruins of former Los Angeles, in a time when North America has become three countries all at war: the Republic, the Colonies and the Patriots. In the Republic, June of the elites and Day, the country's most wanted criminal become unlikely partners.

Other books in the series:
  Prodigy

NORTHERN LIGHTS/GOLDEN COMPASS • Philip Pullman

Lyra Belacqua and Will Parry wander through a series of parallel universes. Meet the amazing Lord Asriel, Mrs Coulter, the armoured bear Iorek, the witch Serafina and learn what dust is and why daemons are important!

Other books in the His Dark Materials series:
  The Subtle Knife
  The Amber Spyglass

THE BLUE SWORD • Robert McKinley

Harry Crewe is an orphan girl who comes to live in Damar, the desert country shared by the Homelanders and the secretive, magical Hillfolk. She lives an ordinary life till she is is kidnapped by Corlath, the Hillfolk king.

Other books in the Damar series:

The Hero and the Crown

Other books by the author:

The Stone Fey

A Knot in the Grain: And Other Stories

ASSASSIN'S APPRENTICE • Robin Hobb

Fitz, son of Chivalry Farseer, is a royal bastard and friendless and undesired. He has a unique skill and after meeting with the king who is worried about the threat to the kingdom and its people, he begins his training to become an assassin.

Other books in the Farseer trilogy:

Royal Assassin

Assassin's Quest

THE UNICORN EXPEDITION AND OTHER STORIES • Satyajit Ray

Professor Shonku believes that unicorns exist, unless it can be proved otherwise. Charles Willard, a deceased fellow scientist claimed to have seen some in Tibet, so when an expedition to Tibet is organized, Shonku grabs the opportunity.

Other books in the series:

The Diary of a Space Traveller and Other Stories

ENCHANTRESS FROM THE STARS • Sylvia Louise Engdahl

Elana is not supposed to to be on the ship that travels to Anrecians, who they must protect against the Empire who wants to colonise them. Elana befriends Georyn who believes she is an enchantress from the stars and together they try to slay the Dragon of the Empire.

Other books in the Elana series:
>   The Far Side of Evil

UNDER THE NEVER SKY • Veronica Rossi

Aria is exiled from Reverie because of a fire that killed her best friend and two other boys. The Death Shop is a wasteland and she will die soon. Then Aria meets an outsider named Perry and he is her only hope for survival.

Other books in the Under the Never Sky series:
>   Roar and Liv
>   Through the Ever Light
>   Into the Still Blue

MEET THE AUTHOR
J.K. ROWLING

She is the super successful author of the Harry Potter series, which has won multiple awards and sold more than four hundred million copies becoming one of the highest selling book series in history.

Rowling conceived the idea for the book on a train ride from Manchester to London in 1990.

The series consists of seven novels that chronicle the adventures of boy wizard Harry Potter and his friends as they pursue their studies at the Hogwarts School of Witchcraft and Wizardry. Lord Voldermort wants control of the whole world and Harry Potter stands in his way.

Books in the Harry Potter series:
- Harry Potter and The Philosopher's Stone
- Harry Potter and The Chamber of Secrets
- Harry Potter and The Prisoner of Azkaban
- Harry Potter and The Goblet of Fire
- Harry Potter and The Order of the Phoenix
- Harry Potter and The Half-blood Prince
- Harry Potter and The Deathly Hallows

Other books about the Harry Potter universe:
- Fantastic Beasts and Where to Find Them
- Quidditch Through The Ages
- The Tales of Beedle the Bard

YOUR FANTASY CHECKLIST

List down the books as you read them. Also rate them and share the ratings with your friends!

Rating scale
- Absolutely Smashing—4
- Very Good—3
- Strictly OK—2
- Did Not Like It One Bit—1

Read the Book	Rating

Growing Up

Friendships, heartbreaks, loss, school and parent problems, each of these books will help you connect with some issues you or your friends may face!

LEVEL 1

THE LUCKIEST GIRL IN THE SCHOOL • Angela Brazil
Winona is an average student but manages to win a scholarship to get through school. She works hard, but bears a terrible guilt.
Other books by the author:
There are more than sixty books by the author, some of which are:
> The Nicest Girl in School
> For the Sake of School
> A Popular Schoolgirl
> A Fourth Form Friendship

FIRST TERM AT TREBIZON • Anne Digby
Rebecca Mason joins the famous boarding school for girls. She makes an enemy of the powerful prefect Elizabeth and unwittingly starts a major row.
Other books in the Trebizon series:
There are many books in the series, some of which are
> Second Term at Trebizon
> Summer Term at Trebizon

Boy Trouble at Trebizon
More Trouble at Trebizon

THE JENNINGS SERIES • Anthony Buckeridge

The Jennings stories are all set in a boarding school, Linbury Court Preparatory. Jennings is impulsive and his best friend Darbishire is cautious. The duo often find themselves in situations they would rather not be in.

Some books in the Jennings series:
There are twenty-five books in the series, some of which are

Jennings Goes to School
Jennings' Little Hut
Jennings and Darbishire
Jennings' Diary

CARBONEL: THE KING OF CATS • Barbara Sleigh

Rosemary decides to help supplement her mother's income by cleaning houses in the summer. Instead, she gets saddled with a cat who is royalty and expects to be waited upon all the time.

Other books in the series:

The Kingdom of Carbonel
Carbonel and Calidor, Being the Further Adventures of a Royal Cat

PIRATES • Celia Rees

Nancy Kington loses her father and is sent off to live on the family plantation at Jamaica. She is horrified at the treatment of slaves and disgusted with her brother who wants to marry her off. So Nancy and a slave, Minerva, run away and join a band of pirates.

Other books by the author:

Every Step You Take

Colour Her Dead
The Truth Out There
The Celia Rees Supernatural Trilogy

THE WATER BABIES: A FAIRY TALE FOR A LAND BABY • Charles Kingsley

Tom works as a chimney sweep and leads a harsh life. He runs away from the house when he is accused of being a thief. He plunges into water and is transformed into a four-inch water baby.

GAY-NECK: THE STORY OF A PIGEON • Dhan Gopal Mukerji

This is the life story of a pigeon—his experiences against a hawk, getting shot and being healed by a lama's wisdom.

THE SHEEP-PIG • Dick King-Smith

Farmer Hoggett has no use for a pig he wins at the local fair, but his wife thinks it would be great to fatten the pig for Christmas. However, Babe, the pig, has other plans. He wants to be a sheep-dog, and Farmer Hoggett enters him into the county sheep-dog trials.

Other books by the author:
   Ace, The Very Important Pig
   A Mouse Called Wolf
   Martin's Mice
   Pigs Might Fly
   The Water Horse

CHARLOTTE'S WEB • E.B. White

The memorable story of Wilbur, a little pig who befriends Charlotte the spider, and goes on to become the prize-winning

pig in the county instead of pork on someone's table.
Other books by the author:
   Stuart Little

POLLYANNA • Eleanor H. Porter
The orphan Pollyanna had the Glad Game that helps her look at everything in life in a positive manner. Soon she wins the hearts of the miserable folk in her stern aunt's town and helps them see the good in everything.

THE SCHOOL AT THE CHALET • Elinor M. Brent-Dyer
Madge Bettany decides to start a school to generate additional income and take care of her unwell sister, Joey. The school is set in a chalet in the Austrian Alps and soon a sanatorium for tuberculosis patients is built not far away from the school.
There are sixty novels in the series and some of the books are:
   Jo of the Chalet School
   The Princess of the Chalet School
   The Head-Girl of the Chalet School
   The Rivals of the Chalet School
   Eustacia Goes to the Chalet School

MISTER GOD, THIS IS ANNA • Fynn
Anna was only four years old when Fynn found her on London's fog-shrouded docks. He took her home and his life changed for the better—forever.
Other books in the series:
   Anna's Book
   Anna and the Black Knight

THE RAILWAY CHILDREN • Edith Nesbit

When Father is falsely accused of selling state secrets to Russia and imprisoned, the family with three children moves to the country. They live in 'Three Chimneys', a house near the railway. The railway station and lines become their playground.

Other books by the author:
   Five Children and It
   The Story of the Treasure Seekers
   The Wouldbegoods

BILLY BUNTER OF GREYFRIARS SCHOOL • Frank Richards

Bunter is not the kind of person you would expect, or want to find in an English public school. He is mean, greedy, dishonest and self-centred.

Other Billy Bunter books:
   Billy Bunter's Banknote
   Billy Bunter's Burning Out
   Billy Bunter in Brazil
   Billy Bunter's Christmas Party
   Billy Bunter's Benefit
   Billy Bunter among the Cannibals

MEET THE AUTHOR
ENID BLYTON

She is a well-known British children's writers. Blyton wrote more than 800 books over a period of forty years. Her books have sold over six hundred million copies and have been translated into ninety languages. She wrote adventure novels, novels on schools, fantasy and sometimes magic, too.

Noddy is one of the most loved characters for young

children. He stays in Toyland and drives a red and yellow taxi. The wooden boy has wonderful friends with whom he has many adventures.

Some of Enid Blyton's famous series are:
  Famous Five
  Secret Seven
  The Five Find-Outers
  The Malory Towers
  St Clare's
  The Naughtiest Girl
  The Magic Faraway Tree

BAMBI • Felix Salten

Bambi is a young roe deer who lives in the jungle with his mother. A moving story of growing up, love, separation, experiencing death and learning to survive in the dangerous jungle.

THE SECRET GARDEN • Frances Hodgson Burnett

Orphaned Mary Lennox comes to live at her uncle's great house on Yorkshire Moors. She is sour and unaffectionate. But Mary changes slowly when she discovers the secret garden and her cousin Colin.

Other books by the author:
  A Little Princess
  Little Lord Fauntleroy
  The Lost Prince
  Sara Crewe, Or What Happened at Miss Minchin's

BLUBBER • Judy Blume

Blubber is a good name for her, says a note about Linda. Linda is bullied in her class by a number of girls, but equations change

between classmates all the time!
Other books by the author:
She has written many books for children and teenagers, some of these are:
> Tiger Eyes
> Are You There God? It's Me, Margaret
> Forever
> Iggie's House

HARRIET THE SPY • Louise Fitzhugh

What would happen if your friends and classmates discover the diary in which you write brutally honest notes about them? Harriet M. Welsch is a spy and she has to face the consequences of her diary being discovered, of losing friends and making many enemies and of trying to make amends.
Other books in the Harriet the Spy series:
> The Long Secret
> Sport

SIDEWAYS STORIES FROM WAYSIDE SCHOOL • Louis Sachar

Wayside School was built with one classroom on top of another, thirty stories high. A teacher who turns her students into apples and is eaten up by one and another who thinks the students are actually monkeys…strange things happen in this weird school.
Other books in the Wayside School series:
> Wayside School is Falling Down
> Wayside School Gets a Little Stranger
> Sideways Arithmetic from Wayside School
> More Sideways Arithmetic from Wayside School

BALLET SHOES • Noel Streatfeild
Ballet Shoes tells the story of Pauline, Petrova and Posy Fossil, who were adopted as babies by Great Uncle Matthew. The three girls meet many interesting characters who are taken in as boarders to supplement the family income. And each girl discovers her own unique talent.

Other books by the author:
Noel Streatfeild has written many *Shoes* books, some of which are:
- Tennis Shoes
- Theater Shoes
- Party Shoes
- Skating Shoes

JENNIE • Paul Gallico
Imagine getting knocked down by a car and waking up as a cat! That is what happened to Peter, and he does not know how to behave in the feline world.

MATILDA • Roald Dahl
Matilda Wormwood is an extraordinary child born to unpleasant parents who don't think too much of her. Underestimating Matilda proves expensive for the parents and the terrible headmistress Miss Trunchbull.

WHAT KATY DID AT SCHOOL • Susan Coolidge
At sixteen, Katy is too serious and grown-up and her father wants to correct that. So off goes Katy with her sister Clover to a boarding school.

Other books by the author:
- What Katy Did

THE STORY-CATCHER • Varsha Seshan
A young girl has to write a story for school with the four words—fire, giant, colour and invisible. And when words start flowing, stories start coming to her too.

THE BLACK STALLION • Walter Farley
Young Alec Ramsay is stranded on a desert island after a shipwreck. His only companion is an Arabian stallion. The two help each other survive and a strong emotional bond is forged between them.

Other books in The Black Stallion series:
- The Black Stallion Returns
- Son of the Black Stallion
- The Island Stallion
- The Black Stallion and Satan
- The Black Stallion's Blood Bay Colt

A SWARM IN MAY • William Mayne
John Owen realizes that he is the youngest Singing Boy in the Choir School. That means he is also a Beekeeper and must sing a solo in the Cathedral. He manages to extricate himself from that task and discovers something in the Cathedral's towers that has been baffling people for years.

Other books by the author:
- Candlefasts
- Cathedral Wednesday
- The Incline
- The Hob Stories

MEET THE AUTHOR
MARK TWAIN

Samuel Langhorne Clemens was better known by his pen name, Mark Twain. He is considered to be one of the greatest humorists of his age.

In *The Adventures of Tom Sawyer*, Tom tries to impress Becky Thatcher, and looks for buried treasure. He runs away and returns to testify at his own death in the court.

Huckleberry Finn thinks that blacks are slaves and therefore his property. He considers them less human, but then meets Jim, a black man.

LEVEL 2

VILLAGE BY THE SEA • Anita Desai

Hari hates his life. His mother is bedridden and he has to pay off the debts of his drunkard father and also look after his three siblings. So Hari leaves his fishing village and runs away to Bombay.

THE SISTERHOOD OF THE TRAVELING PANTS • Ann Brashares

Carmen buys a pair of second-hand jeans at a thrift store and discovers that they fit and flatter her. They also fit her three best friends perfectly well even though they are all of different shapes and sizes. The girls are travelling separately all summer and decide to form a sisterhood of the traveling pants.

Other books in The Sisterhood of the Traveling Pants series:

> The Second Summer of the Sisterhood
> The Third Summer of the Sisterhood

The Fourth Summer of the Sisterhood
Sisterhood Everlasting

THE DIARY OF A YOUNG GIRL • Anne Frank
It is 1942, and a thirteen-year-old Jewish girl flees her home in Amsterdam and goes into hiding. The Nazis have occupied Holland and their lives are in danger. Anne spends her last years in the attic before being sent to a concentration camp and dying there. This is her diary.

CALL IT COURAGE • Armstrong Sperry
Mafatu is the son of a chief and is afraid of the sea. This makes him a subject of scorn in the tribe and Mafatu decides to take a canoe and see where it will take him. Finally a changed Mafatu returns home.

Other books by the author:
Storm Canvas
The Rain Forest

HUSH, HUSH • Becca Fitzpatrick
Nora's best friend Vee is constantly trying to fix her up with boys, but Nora is not interested. Then she meets Patch and is inexplicably drawn to him.

Other books in the Hush, Hush series:
Crescendo
Silence
Finale

THE REFUGEE BOY • Benjamin Zephaniah
Alem's father takes him to London for his fourteenth birthday. But Alem wakes up to realize that his father has left him. Alem's

parents decided to leave him in London because they thought it would be safer for him than the war-torn Ethiopia.
Other books by the author:
Face

KIRA-KIRA • Cynthia Kadohata
'Kira-Kira' means glittering, and that's how Katie Takeshima's sister Lynn makes everything appear. But then Lynn falls sick, and as her family struggles to cope, it falls on Katie to remind them that there is always something kira-kira in the future.
Other books by the author:
Cracker: The Best Dog in Vietnam
Weedflower
Outside Beauty
A Million Shades of Grey

HUNT FOR THE MIRACLE HERB • Deepa Agarwal
Fourteen-year-old Ajay, twelve-year-old Rina and nine-year-old Geeti go to spend a holiday with their Uncle Raj in the Kumaon Hills. Uncle is a botanist and among other things, wants to find the miracle herb that can cure a terrible disease.
Other books by the author:
Caravan to Tibet
Rajula and the Web of Danger

NATIONAL VELVET • Enid Bagnold
Fourteen-year-old Velvet is the plainest of her sisters and her father worries that she will not find herself a husband. She wins a horse in a raffle, trains it and herself to enter the Grand National steeplechase—and wins it.

THE PROPHECY OF THE STONES • Flavia Bujor
In a magical realm, three teenage girls—Jade, Opal and Amber—meet as strangers who must travel together. They are sent on a journey, with only magical stones, to fulfil their destiny.

MINN OF THE MISSISSIPPI • H.C. Holling
Minn is a turtle who begins her life as an egg at the source of the Mississippi river. Her journey down the river takes us through the landscape till the Gulf of Mexico.

MY SIDE OF THE MOUNTAIN • Jean Craighead George
Sam runs away from home for adventure and independence. He spends a year in a forested area around New York and learns to be independent, self-reliant and also the meaning of companionship.

STARGIRL • Jerry Spinelli
Stargirl is an unusual girl. Homeschooled till Grade 10, she enters high school and immediately charms her way into the hearts of all the students. But the enchantment does not last long and the students clamour to make her fit in.
Other books in the Stargirl series:
   Love, Stargirl

MARLEY AND ME • John Grogan
Newly-married John and Jenny prepare for a lifetime together and get Marley, a puppy, home. Marley turns their lives upside down.

FLUTE IN THE FOREST • Leela Gour Broome
Atiya ventures quite often into the forest where her father is a forest officer. She is afflicted with polio, and one day hears the

notes of a flute. In secret she learns to play the flute and makes many friends in the forest.

FALLEN • Lauren Kate
Lucinda 'Luce' Price, is sent to the Sword and Cross Reform School after she is accused of murdering a boy by starting a fire. She meets Daniel and is mysteriously drawn to him. He makes it clear he does not want to associate with her, but she is unable to withdraw.

Other books in the Fallen series:
- Torment
- Passion
- Rapture
- Fallen in Love

Other books by the author:
- The Fallen Shorts series
- The Betrayal of Natalie Hargrove

MEET THE AUTHOR
RUSKIN BOND

One of India's most loved writers, Ruskin Bond has written novels, stories, poetry for children and adults alike for over six decades now. He has been felicitated with numerous awards including the Sahitya Akademi award and most of his books have been in print since they were published.

The Room on the Roof, written when he was seventeen, is the story of Rusty, an Anglo-Indian boy who lives unhappily with his stepfather till one day he walks out of home and starts living among his friends from the bazaar.

Some of Bond's other best known works are:
- Rusty, the Boy from the Hills

Panther's Moon
Dust on the Mountain and Other Stories
Angry River
Blue Umbrella
Tigers for Dinner

ANNE OF GREEN GABLES • L.M. Montgomery
The series is about Anne, an orphan who is sent to a middle-aged brother and sister who have a farm on Prince Edward Island and want to adopt a boy to help them.
Some other books in the series:
  Anne of Avonlea
  Anne of the Island
  Anne of Windy Poplars
  Anne's House of Dreams
Other books by the author:
  The Emily trilogy
  Pat of Silver Bush
  The Story Girl

HOLES • Louis Sachar
Stanley Yelnat inherits his family's bad fortune. He ends up in a juvenile detention centre for a crime he did not commit and is forced to dig a hole everyday before breakfast. The warden claims it is for character building, but Stanley suspects otherwise.
Other books in the series:
  Small Steps
Other books by the author:
  The Wayside School series

THE GIRL MECHANIC OF WANZHOU • Marjorie Sayer
Twelve-year-old Zun, growing up in Wanzhou in 1902, has an envious childhood. She works with her dad who designs bicycles and loves all things mechanical. She learns reading and writing from her mother. Her happy world is destroyed when her father is murdered.

THIS SCHOOL IS DRIVING ME CRAZY • Nat Hentoff
Twelve-year-old Sam is not having a great time at school. He has the knack of attracting trouble and his father happens to be the headmaster of the school.
Other books by the author:
   Jazz Country
   In the Country of Ourselves

ESPERANZA RISING • Pam Munoz Ryan
Esperanza leads a life of luxury on her ranch in Mexico. She and her mother are forced to escape to California during the Great Depression and Esperanza learns to live in a camp for Mexican farm workers.
Other books by the author:
   Becoming Naomi Leon
   The Dreamer
   Riding Freedom
   Paint the Wind

NO GUNS AT MY SON'S FUNERAL • Paro Anand
Aftab is a regular Kashmiri teenager who loves cricket, his family and friends. But he leads a double life and is in awe of Akram who leads a group of fledgling terrorists.

Other books by the author:
- I'm not Butter Chicken and Other Stories for Teenagers
- Weed
- Wingless
- The World's Worst Genius

A MONSTER CALLS • Patrick Ness

Conor is distressed. He knows his mother is very ill but nobody tells him the truth and kids in school tease him about his mother going bald. A yew tree outside his window transforms into a monster who helps him cope.

Other books by the author:
- The Chaos Walking series
- The Crash of Hennington

SWAMI AND FRIENDS • R.K. Narayan

The stories revolve around a little boy called Swami and his many adventures in the fictional town of Malgudi. Swami does not really enjoy school and often gets into trouble there and with his strict father. The book revisits the innocent days of childhood with doses of humour and adventure.

Other books by the author:
- Malgudi Days
- The Talkative Man
- Guide

MISS PEREGRINE'S HOME FOR PECULIAR CHILDREN • Ransom Riggs

Sixteen-year-old Jacob has a nervous breakdown after his grandfather is brutally murdered. He goes back to an abandoned orphanage on a Welsh island where his grandfather spent time before enlisting in the war. Jacob finds out that the children who stayed here were not only peculiar, but quite dangerous too—and may still be alive.

STALKY & CO. • Rudyard Kipling
A set of stories set in a boarding school that feature Stalky and Co. These boys are seasoned rebels, often indulging in violence and playing the fool.

BETWEEN SHADES OF GRAY • Ruta Sepetys
The Soviet secret police barge into fifteen-year-old Lina's home in 1941 and the family gets separated. Lina, her mom and brother are sent to a camp in Siberia where they must dig beets to survive, and her father goes to a prison camp. Will the family ever be together again?

BLOOMABILITY • Sharon Creech
Dinnie Doone is used to a nomadic life as her family moves around a lot in the US. Then she is whisked away to Switzerland to a school where her uncle is the headmaster. She discovers life, its possibilities and herself!

Other books by the author:
- The Great Unexpected
- Love That Dog
- Ruby Holler
- Chasing Redbird

THE ARTICHOKE HEARTS • Sita Brahmachari
This is a book about a twelve-year-old girl whose life is being turned upside down. Her Nana is dying of cancer and Mira is unable to share her feelings with anyone. In comes Pat Print,

the author who runs a writing group at school. Mira learns to articulate her feelings and share them, and comes to term with life and death.
Other books by the author:
Jasmine Skies

HOW I TAUGHT MY GRANDMOTHER TO READ AND OTHER STORIES • Sudha Murty

This collection of stories is about the simple events of everyday life, and the value of honesty, gratitude and love–that never go out of date.
Other books by the author:
Wise and Otherwise
The Magic Drum and Other Stories
Grandma's Bag of Stories

FLIPPED • Wendelin Van Draanen

Juli Baker has liked Bryce forever and stalks him and wants him to be friends with her. Shy Bryce is furious and uncomfortable with the attention and runs away from her all the time. In grade eight, Juli begins to think Bryce is not really the nice guy she thought he was and starts to ignore him. But Bryce now begins to like Juli.

MEET THE AUTHOR
LOUISA MARY ALCOTT

Louisa grew up among many well-known intellectuals of her time, such as Emerson and Thoreau. Since her family suffered severe financial difficulties, Louisa worked to help support her family from an early age. She also wrote under the pen name of A.M. Barnard.

Little Women is loosely based on Louisa's childhood experiences with her three sisters. It follows the lives of four sisters—Meg, Jo, Beth and Amy March. It was a unique novel of the time and is still as well-loved today.

Good Wives follows *Little Women* and the March sisters, who are also featured in *Little Men* and *Jo's Boys*.

Other books by the author:

An Old Fashioned Girl
Eight Cousins
Rose in Bloom
Under the Lilacs

LEVEL 3

THE RAINBOW TROOPS • Andrea Hirata

Published in Indonesia in 2005, this autobiographical debut novel sold more than five million copies. Ikal is a student at the poorest village school on the Indonesian island of Belitong, where graduating from sixth grade is considered a remarkable achievement. His school is under constant threat of closure. An engrossing depiction of a milieu we have never encountered before, bursting with charm and verve.

THE CENTRE OF THE WORLD • Andreas Steinhofel

Glass is a strange mother to her seventeen-year-old twins. All that Phil and Dianne know is that their father was Number Three on the long list of lovers their mother had. This causes a problem with the critical townspeople but Glass is strong and inspiring and teaches her children how to lead their lives.

THE LOUDEST FIRECRACKER • Arun Krishnan

It's a cricket match between India and Pakistan and as the anxiety becomes palpable in the final over, ten-year-old Siddharth sets off a firecracker. Siddharth's life changes in that blast, and he must make meaning of it.

GO ASK ALICE • Beatrice Sparks

A diary of an anonymous girl whose life goes into a downward spiral after she starts taking drugs. A poignant account of losing it all to drugs—youth, innocence and ultimately life itself.

IMPULSE • Ellen Hopkins

Three young children come to Aspen Springs to recover and heal. All three tried to end their lives—one by pulling the trigger, another by swallowing pills and the third by slashing her wrists. Can they help each other?

Other books by the author:
  Perfect
  Tilt

TO SIR, WITH LOVE • E.R. Braithwaite

A teacher who takes up a teaching assignment in a tough London school slowly comes to realize that the rough kids there need his help. He works at breaking the barriers of racial prejudices, teaching the children values and above all self-respect.

PSYCHE IN A DRESS • Francesca Lia Block

Psyche has known Love—he comes to her every night and tells her many stories. The only deal is that she must not ask to see his face. Goaded by her sisters, Psyche lights a candle to see Love, and loses him. As Psyche sets out to seek him, she experiences the lives of the many mythical figures Love had told her about.

IF I STAY • Gayle Forman
Seventeen-year-old Mia gets into a terrible car accident and is in coma. She has an out-of-body experience and watches her family and friends cope with their grief. Will Mia decide to wake up or will she decide to pass on?
Other books in the series:
   Where She Went

GOODBYE, MR CHIPS • James Hilton
The work depicts the career of a gentle schoolteacher at an English public school. Mr Chips taught at the Brookfield School for forty-three years and overcame his shyness to connect with the students and guide and discipline them.

MANIAC MAGEE • Jerry Spinelli
There is racial tension between the black Eastenders and the white Westenders at Two Hills. In comes Maniac Magee, and through his attempts tries to get both the sides to understand each other.

THE CATASTROPHIC HISTORY OF YOU AND ME • Jess Rothenberg
Brie's heart breaks—literally and figuratively—when her boyfriend tells her that he does not love her any more. Now dead and gone, in the company of her new guide Patrick, Brie watches her family unravel, and finally understands Jacob, her boyfriend.

THE BOY IN THE STRIPED PYJAMAS • John Boyne
Nine-year-old Bruno is the son of a Nazi official and enjoys his friends and life at Berlin. He knows nothing of the Holocaust or

the Final Solution when his family moves next to a concentration camp. Bruno meets Shmuel who lives on the other side of the fence, wears striped pyjamas and becomes his only friend in that desolate place.

LOOKING FOR ALASKA • John Green
Miles Halter, fascinated with famous last words and bored of his life at home, moves into a boarding school. There he meets the clever and funny Alaska Young. Will she catapult him into the Great Perhaps?

Other books by the author:
> The Fault in Our Stars
> An Abundance of Katherines
> Let it Snow—with Maureen Johnson and Lauren Myracle
> Paper Towns

LEVERAGE • Joshua Cohen
The Oregrove High School football players are considered gods and no one messes with them. But when things go too far, Danny, the gymnast and his new friend Kurt the fullback on the football team, decide that enough is enough.

HOMEWARD BOUND • Lawrence Bransby
The end of apartheid seems imminent in South Africa, and it is pretty certain that schools will be de-segregated. What will happen to the first black child in an all-white boarding school?

DEAD TO YOU • Lisa McMann
Ethan, now sixteen, was abducted when he was seven. He returns home and at first, his return is nothing short of a miracle, and then things begin to unravel.

Other books by the author:
- Wake
- Fade
- Gone
- The Unwanteds
- Cryer's Cross

THE BOOK THIEF • Markus Zusak

Leisel loves to read and the love for books helps her tide over the violence around her. She loses most of the people she loves in the World War and many years later, when Death comes for her, he comes with her little diary titled, The Book Thief.

Other books by the author:
- The Messenger
- The Underdog
- Fighting Ruben Wolfe
- When Dogs Cry

WICKED LOVELY • Melissa Marr

Keenan woos Aislinn who he believes is the one who will return Summer to the faeries. Aislinn is special, she can see faeries and other-world creatures. Her safe haven is her best friend and crush Seth, and his home fashioned from a train car. Can she resist Keenan?

Other books in the series:
- Ink Exchange
- Fragile Eternity
- Radiant Shadows
- Darkest Mercy

ROLL OF THUNDER, HEAR MY CRY • Mildred Taylor
Nine-year-old Cassie Logan's world is torn asunder when she is confronted with racial hatred. Amidst deprivation, poverty, illness and betrayal, Cassie learns the meaning of bigotry as well as family love.

Other books in the series:
- Song of the Trees
- Let the Circle be Unbroken
- The Road to Memphis
- The Land

BURGER WUSS • M.T. Anderson
Anthony is in love with Diana and believes she is the right one for him. Then a boy steals her away. Anthony is furious and takes up a job in a fast food joint where the other boy is a star performer. Anthony will not let him get away with his girl.

Other books by the author:
- Feed
- Thirsty
- The Astonishing Life of Octavia Nothing

MIKE: A PUBLIC SCHOOL STORY • P.G. Wodehouse
Mike comes from a cricketing family and joins a boarding school where his brothers are cricketing stars. He gets into trouble a lot and plays loads of cricket too. Mike is to become the captain of the cricketing team when his father gets enraged by his report card and moves him to a smaller school called Sedleigh where he meets Psmith.

Other books by the author:
- The Pothunters
- A Prefect's Uncle

Tales of St Austin's
The Gold Bat

THE PERKS OF BEING A WALLFLOWER • Stephen Chbosky

Charlie's best friend has commited suicide and now, a year later, Charlie has to attend high school all alone. His diary tells us about what it's like in high school—including the world of drugs, sex and the Rocky Horror Picture Show.

MBA AT 16 • Subroto Bagchi

Get a teen MBA through this book. How does the corporate world work and what makes an entrepreneur successful? Can you create a business that touches everyone's life and is there merit in becoming a social entrepreneur. Discover all this and more.

TOM BROWN'S SCHOOLDAYS • Thomas Hughes

The experiences of Tom Brown at the Rugby School and his transformation from a thoughtless boy into a selfless, mature young man.

Other books in the series:

Tom Brown at Oxford

GIFTS • Ursula K. Le Guin

The Uplanders possess gifts that protect them from other feuding magic tribes. These gifts range from twisting limbs to inflicting wasting diseases. Orrec's father can 'unmake' and he expects his son to inherit his gift. But Orrec's gift seems wild and uncontrollable.

Other books in the Annals of the Western Shore series:

Voices
Powers

MEET THE AUTHOR
JACQUELINE WILSON

Jacqueline Wilson has written a number of books for children. Her novels talk about many aspects of life including adoption and divorce.

The Story of Tracy Beaker is about young Tracy who creates a fanciful world to help her cope with the harsh reality of her real world. She claims her mother is a Hollywood actress and therefore is too busy to spend time with her, whereas her mother is actually indifferent to her.

Some of Jacqueline's well-known books are:
- Double Act
- Girls in Love
- Vicky Angel
- Video Rose
- The Mum-Minder
- The Illustrated Mum
- The Lottie Project
- Buried Alive
- Lizzie Zipmouth
- Take a Good Look
- My Brother Bernadette
- How to Survive a Summer Camp
- The Worry Website

YOUR GROWING UP CHECKLIST

List down the books as you read them. Also rate them and share the ratings with your friends!

Rating scale

Absolutely Smashing—4

Very Good—3
Strictly OK—2
Did Not Like It One Bit—1

Read the Book	Rating

Historical Fiction and Books on History

Stories set in various time periods—from pre-historic times to Roman, Victorian, Mughal and others—that transport you to a different world. Read about politics, intrigue and lives of people through the ages, in stories that are spellbinding!

LEVEL 1

ATISA AND THE SEVEN WONDERS • Anuradha Kumar
A flying machine crashes near Atisa's home. While tinkering with it, Atisa takes off unexpectedly and has an incredible adventure visiting the Seven Wonders of the World.
Other books with Atisa:
   Atisa and his Flying Machine: Adventures with Hieun Tsang
Other books by the author:
   In the Country of Gold-Digging Ants: 2000 Years of Travel in India
   Puffin Lives: Subhash Chandra Bose
   On Top of the World (with Arjun Vajpai)
   Mythquest: Mythical Animals (nine books)
   The Mahatma and the Monkeys
   Mythquest: Asuras (nine books)

FIRE, BED, AND BONE • Henrietta Branford
An old hunting dog lives a good life with his masters. It is 1381 and his owners are imprisoned for attending revolutionary meetings. The dog helps find safe homes for their children, lets them know the children are safe and tries to find a solution.

Other books by the author:
  The Fated Sky
  The Theft of Thor's hammer
  Dimanche Diller

CORAM BOY • Jamila Gavin
The Coram Man collects orphans and abandoned babies and delivers them to a safe life at the Coram Hospital in London. Is he really a good Samaritan?

Other books by the author:
  The Wormholers
  Daisy and the Intergalactic Travelling Salesman
  The Surya Trilogy
  The Magic Orange Tree and Other Haitian Folktales

TIME CAT • Lloyd Alexander
Jason's cat is an unusual one. It can talk and can visit nine lives. So when an upset Jason wants to escape his reality, the cat Gareth takes him travelling through time!

Other books by the author:
  Taran Wanderer
  Westmark
  The Castle of Llyr
  The High King

THE RIVER BETWEEN US • Richard Peck
1861: Civil War is imminent and Tilly Pruitt's brother Noah wants to go and fight, while Tilly, her sister and their mother struggle to make ends meet. Two women come on a steamboat bound for St Louis and Tilly's mother takes them in as boarders. The Pruitts' lives are changed forever.

Other books by the author:
    A Long Way from Chicago
    A Year from Down Yonder
    A Season for Gifts
    The Teacher's Funeral: A Comedy in Three Parts

A WAY THROUGH THE SEA • Robert Elmer
The first in the Young Underground series, the novel is about Peter and Elise, eleven-year-old twins. In 1943, Danes struggled to save Danish Jews from the Nazis. The twins try to help their Jewish friend Henrik escape to Sweden.

Other books in the Young Underground series:
    Beyond the River
    Into the Flames
    Far From the Storm
    Chasing the Wind
    A Light in the Castle
    Follow the Star
    Touch the Sky

THE AWESOME EGYPTIANS • Terry Deary
Ancient Egypt was not only about pyramids and mummies. In this amazing book, find out how mummies were made, if the pyramids are indeed magical and how Egyptians lived. Along with that read all the horrible and gross bits that usual history

books generally leave out.
Other books in the Horrible Histories series:
There are many amazing books in the series, some of which are:

> The Groovy Greeks
> The Rotten Romans
> The Terrible Tudors
> The Vicious Vikings
> The Angry Aztecs

LEVEL 2

A REALLY SHORT HISTORY OF NEARLY EVERYTHING • Bill Bryson

In this exciting edition for younger readers, Bryson covers the wonder and mysteries of time and space, the frequently bizarre and often obsessive scientists and the methods they used, the crackpot theories which held sway for far too long, the extraordinary accidental discoveries which suddenly advanced whole areas of science when the people were actually looking for something else.

MARY, BLOODY MARY • Carolyn Meyer

Princess Mary was the daughter of Catherine of Aragon and King Henry VII and she was to be engaged to the king of France. However, all was not well in the court. Her father wants to divorce her mother ostensibly because there is no male heir and because he wants Anne Boleyn.

Other books in the Young Royals series:

> Beware, Princess Elizabeth
> Doomed Queen Anne
> Patience, Princess Catherine

Duchessina
The Bad Queen: Rules and Instructions for Marie Antoinette

VICTORY SONG • Chitra Banerjee Divakaruni
Neela is a village girl in Bengal. The freedom movement rages in India and she finds herself caught between the village traditions and her sympathy with the freedom fighters. When her father disappears to fight with them, she risks her life and reputation to try to find him, and travels all the way to distant Calcutta.

SOLDIER BOYS • Dean Hughes
Dieter is a young German, determined to prove himself at war and Spence wants to be a hero in the Allied forces. Their paths cross when Spence helps an injured Dieter cross the enemy lines so he can be attended to, but is fatally shot himself.

THE WITCH OF BLACKBIRD POND • Elizabeth George Speare
After her grandfather's death, Kit leaves Barbados for New England. The life here is different from the one she was used to in Barbados and Kit finds it difficult to fit in. She becomes friends with Hannah, an outsider. Hannah is branded a witch, and Kit has to choose between Hannah and losing everything in her life.
Other books by the author:
The Sign of the Beaver
The Bronze Bow
Calico Captive
The Prospering

THE GOLDEN GOBLET • Eloise Jarvis McGraw
Ranofer is happy to apprentice with his father, a famous goldsmith

who makes jewelry for royalty in Egypt. Then his father dies and his cruel half-brother Gebu takes away all that is precious to Ranofer. Will Ranofer ever be a goldsmith?

Other books by the author:
 The Striped Ships
 Moccasin Trail
 The Moorchild
 Mara, a Daughter of the Nile
 Greensleeves
 The Seventeenth Swap
 A Really Weird Summer

THE RAMSAY SCALLOP • Frances Temple

In 1299, fourteen-year-old Elenor is not looking forward to the return of her fiancé Robert from the Crusades. She fears loss of freedom and confides in the village priest. Robert returns, disillusioned and not ready for Elenor either. They are sent on a pilgrimage together.

Other books by the author:
 The Beduin's Gazelle
 Taste of Salt: A Story of Modern Haiti
 Grab Hands and Run

STEAM PUNK! AN ANTHOLOGY OF FANTASTICALLY RICH AND STRANGE STORIES • edited by Gavin Grant and Kelly Link

Imagine an alternate universe where romance and technology thrive. Meet characters across geographies and times–from the last technocratic ruler standing trial for his crimes in a post-apocalyptic world to ghosts in a Welsh story to children maimed while working in a clockwork factory.

A BOY AT WAR: A NOVEL OF PEARL HARBOUR • Harry Mazer

Adam and his friends Martin and Davi go fishing on a nice sunny Sunday in Honolulu. They admire the US Navy ships including Adam's father's, the *Arizona*. Then the kids watch in horror as Japanese planes fly overhead, shooting down the US Navy ships.

Other books by the author:

Mazer has written about twenty-two novels, some of which are:

    The Last Mission
    The Solid Gold Kid
    The Island Keeper
    Heroes Don't Run
    Show Bound

THE CLAN OF THE CAVE BEAR • Jean Auel

30,000 years ago, five-year-old Ayla lost her family and was found by a group of Neanderthal people who did not care much for her. Only their medicine woman saw Ayla as being worthy of her care.

Other books in the Earth's Children series:

    The Valley of Horses
    The Mammoth Hunters
    The Plains of Passage
    The Shelters of Stone
    The Land of the Painted Caves

THE ART OF KEEPING COOL • Janet Taylor Lisle

Robert lives with his mother and sister in Rhode Islands with his grandparents during World War II. Grandfather controls them with his rage, and Robert uses drawings to create images of things he fears. The whole town is in fear of Nazi submarines offshore and of the reclusive German artist, Abel Hoffman.

Other books by the author:
- Black Duck
- Afternoon of the Elves
- Highway Cats
- The Crying Rocks

MEET THE AUTHOR
ANN RINALDI

Rinaldi got interested in American history when her son Ron became a part of the Revolutionary War re-enactments while at high school. Her first historical novel, *Time Enough for Drums,* was rejected by ten publishers who claimed that children would not want to read history. When the book was finally published, it became an ALA best book. Rinaldi has written a lot of historical fiction ever since.

In *My Father's House*, Oscie Mason is angered by her stepfather's opinions about slavery, the Confederacy and Oscie's world. When he moves the family, Oscie learns about the battles fought inside the home.

Rinaldi has written over forty books, some of which are:
- Nine Days a Queen
- A Break with Charity
- Hang a Thousand Trees with Ribbons
- The Fifth of March: A Story of the Boston Massacre
- A Ride into the Morning: The Story of the Temple Wick
- Finishing Becca
- Time Enough for Drums
- The Second Bend in the River
- A Stitch in Time
- Girl in Blue
- The Last Silk Dress
- Sarah's Ground

MILKWEED • Jerry Spinelli

The young boy calls himself Stopthief because that is what he hears people call him. He lives on the streets of a Warsaw ghetto and is adept at stealing food for himself and the other orphans. And he realizes that as a Jew, invisibility is the best cloak he can wear.

Other books by the author:
- Loser
- Stargirl
- Wringer

STOWAWAY • Karen Hesse

Nick is deperate to get away from his present life. He pays three sailors to hide him as a stowaway on HMS Endeavour. When he is certain that Captain Cook would not take him off the ship, Nick comes out of hiding and is assigned as a helper to the ship's doctor.

Other books by the author:
- Out of the Dust
- Letters from Rifka
- The Music of Dolphins
- Phoenix Rising

PUFFIN LIVES: AKBAR THE MIGHTY EMPEROR • Kavitha Mandana

In this story of the emperor's life, the author describes Akbar's rough, difficult childhood spent on the run; his consolidation of the empire through war and diplomacy; the myriad interesting and entertaining people who made up his court; the strong women of the Mughal household; and finally, the intriguing circumstances under which the crown passed on to his son, Jahangir.

Other books in the Puffin Lives series:
- Ashoka, the Great and Compassionate King, Subhadra Sen Gupta
- Rani Lakshmibai, the Valiant Queen of Jhansi, Deepa Agarwal
- Mahatma Gandhi, the Father of the Nation, Subhadra Sen Gupta
- Netaji Subhas Chandra Bose, the Great Freedom Fighter, Anu Kumar
- Rabindranath Tagore, the Renaissance Man, Monideepa Sahu
- Chanakya, the Master of Statecraft, Deepa Agarwal

DEAD RECKONING: A PIRATE VOYAGE WITH CAPTAIN DRAKE • Laurie Lawlor

Emmet is saved from his fellow villagers by his newly discovered cousin Captain Francis Drake. Emmet goes on Drake's ship as his servant, and sets off on a trading expedition to Alexandria, Tripoli and Constantinople.

Other books by the author:
- Addie Series
- American Sisters Series
- The Two Loves of Will Shakespeare
- He Will Go Fearless
- The School at Crooked Creek

BLOODY JACK: BEING THE ACCOUNT OF THE CURIOUS ADVENTURES OF MARY 'JACKY', FABER SHIP'S BOY • L.A. Meyer

Mary is a scavenger on the mean streets of London and signs up with her gang as ship boys. She becomes Jacky Faber and gets into loads of scraps. But she has a secret to keep—no one must know she is a girl.

Other books in the Bloody Jack series:
There are ten books in the series, some of which are:
> Curse of the Blue Tattoo: Being an Account of the Misadventures of Jacky Faber, Midshipman and Fine Lady
> Under the Jolly Roger: Being an Account of the Further Nautical Adventures of Jacky Faber
> In the Belly of the Bloodhound: Being an Account of a Particularly Peculiar Adventure in the Life of Jacky Faber

NUMBER THE STARS • Lois Lowry

It is 1943 and a time of war shortages and Nazi soldiers in Copenhagen. Ten-year-old Annemarie Johansen and her best friend Ellen Rosen remember their life before things got so bad. Ellen is a Jew and Annemarie's family is determined to protect her from the Nazis.

Other books by the author:
> The Giver series
> Gossamer
> A Summer to Die
> The Silent Boy

THE BOOK OF THE LION • Michael Cadnum

A young apprentice, Edmund, goes on the First Crusade with his master. He is saved from getting his arms hacked off at the order of the Sheriff of Nottingham and accompanies his rescuers Nigel and Rannulf on the journey to the Holy Land and beyond.

Other books in the Crusader trilogy:
> The Leopard Sword
> The Dragon Throne

CLIMBING THE STAIRS • Padma Venkatraman

It is the last days of British occupation in India and Padma lives in Bombay with her parents. Her father supports her dreams to go to college but then disaster strikes. Her father is beaten senseless in a protest rally and the family moves back into the family home at Madras.

THE RUBY IN THE SMOKE • Philip Pullman

Sally Lockhart is determined to solve the mystery surrounding her father's death. 'Seven Blessings' seems to be a fatal blessing because when she asks her father's former associate about it, he dies of a heart attack. Shipping companies, opium gangs and others are out to get her. But the uncommonly pretty Sally is also uncommonly adept in warfare.

Other books in the Sally Lockhart series:
> The Shadow in the North
> The Tiger in the Well
> The Tin Princess

SWORD SONG • Rosemary Sutcliff

Bjarni is banished from his Viking home when he unintentionally kills a man who kicked his dog. The hot-tempered young man becomes a mercenary swordsman and then attaches himself to various Viking leaders in their battles.

Other books by the author:
> Sutcliff wrote many books, some of which are:
> Eagle of the Ninth series
> Arthurian novels
> The High Deeds of Finn MacCool

GIRLS OF INDIA: A MAURYAN ADVENTURE • Subhadra Sen Gupta

Madhura is twelve and lives in the legendary city of Pataliputra during the reign of King Ashoka of the Mauryan dynasty. She works in the palace as the maid and companion of Princess Sanghamitra. She dreams of travelling across the land like her brother Kartik, and growing up to become a soldier. Madhura's dreams suddenly come true as she travels with Kartik from Pataliputra to Ujjaini in a caravan.

Other books in the series:
    A Harappa Adventure, Sunila Gupte
    A Chola Adventure, Anuradha Kumar

Other books by the author:
    Sen Gupta has written a number of books based on history. Some of these are:
    Bishnu the Dhobi Singer
    History, Mystery, Dal, Biryani
    A Clown for Tenali
    Let's Go Time-Travelling
    Saffron, White and Green: The Amazing Story of India's Independence

SECRET OF THE SANDS • Tavius E. and Rai Aren

In the shadow of the Great Sphinx of Giza, two young archeologists stumble upon a chest. It contains cylinders, not made of any known elements, and has scrolls written in an unknown script. What is the deadly secret they hold?

Other books in the series:
    Destiny of the Sands

ANNA OF BYZANTIUM • Tracy Barrett

Anna was a precious child. She was the firstborn and her father's chosen successor to the throne. Then a baby brother is born to her, and her prize catch is snatched away from her.

Other books by the author:

Barrett has written nineteen novels, some of which are:

> The 100-Year-Old Secret
> Dark of the Moon
> King of the Ithaka
> On Etruscan Time
> The Missing Heir

A SPY IN THE HOUSE • Y.S. Lee

Rescued from the gallows in 1850s London, young orphan and thief Mary Quinn is surprised when Anne Treleaven offers her admission to the school she runs. By the time she is seventeen, Mary is bored of learning needlework and embroidery and then Anne tells her the true purpose of the school.

Other books in the The Agency series:

> The Body at the Tower
> The Traitor in the Tunnel
> Rivals in the City

LEVEL 3

RAIDERS FROM THE NORTH • Alex Rutherford

Babur leaves his kingdom at Fergana to make an attempt to conquer India, not to rob it of its riches, but to establish one of the greatest empires of the Middle Ages—the Moghul Empire.

Other books in the Empire of the Moghuls series:

> Brothers at War

Ruler of the World
The Tainted Throne

BRIGHT YOUNG THINGS • Anna Godbersen

1929: Letty Larkspur and Cordelia Grey leave their small town in Ohio and make their way to glittering New York. Cordelia wants to find her bootlegger father, and Letty wants to become a star. Other books in the Bright Young Things series:
Beautiful Days
The Lucky Ones

MEMOIRS OF A GEISHA • Arthur Golden

Sayuri was a young girl when she began her training as a geisha. Her memoirs are about the intense training she went through to become a geisha and her enduring love for a man who might never be hers.

30 PIECES OF SILVER: AN EXTREMELY CONTROVERSIAL HISTORICAL THRILLER • Carolyn McCray

Two research professors set out to find the authentic bone sample from Jesus Christ's remains and there are more than thirty people involved in faking the resurrection of Christ. As the professors travel under the protection of the US Armed forces, Knot, a religious outfit, tails them, determined to keep some things secret.

A TALE OF TWO CITIES • Charles Dickens

A love story and more set in the backdrop of the French Revolution and the anger against the aristocracy in France. Both Sydney Carton and Charles Darney are in love with Lucie Manette, who marries Charles. But Carton proves that his love for Lucie is enduring.

WOLF OF THE PLAINS • Conn Iggulden

Yesugei is the khan of the Mongol 'Wolf', and when he dies, his bondsman Eeluk takes control and leaves the khan's wife, sons and infant daughter to perish in the unforgiving plains. Thus begins the process of nation building by Yesugei's fierce son Temujin, also known as Genghis Khan.

Other books in the Conqueror series:
- Lords of the Bow
- Bones of the Hills
- Empire of Silver
- Conqueror

Other books by the author:
- The Emperor series
- The Dangerous Book for Boys

THE THORN BIRDS • Colleen McCullough

An epic saga set in the Australian outbacks, Meggie Cleary loves the one person she cannot have–the older Ralph de Bricassart. Ralph rises from a parish priest to the inner hallows of the Vatican, but his passion for Meggie is undiminished.

FLASHMAN • George MacDonald Fraser

What happened to the craven Flashy who was expelled from school in *Tom Brown's Schooldays*? He becomes a soldier, and while he quakes with fear in the first Afghanistan war, he still chases women and drinks!

Other books in the Flashman series:
- Flashman
- Royal Flash

Flash for Freedom!
Flashman at the Charge
Flashman in the Great Game

THE TWENTIETH WIFE • Indu Sundaresan
Mehr-un-Nisa was the twentieth wife of Jahangir and one he remained besotted with. The beautiful Mehr-un-Nisa becomes Nur Jahan and rules the Mughal Empire alongside her husband. Other books in the Taj Mahal trilogy:
The Feast of the Roses
Shadow Princess

MYSELF, MY ENEMY • Jean Plaidy
The story of Henrietta Maria, wife of the doomed Charles I. She had a successful and loving marriage with Charles I, but they fought intrigue in their court unaware of the spies like Cromwell in their court.
Other books in the Queens of England series:
The Courts of Love
The Queen's Secret
The Reluctant Queen
The Lady in the Tower
Rose Without a Thorn
In the Shadow of the Crown
Queen of This Realm
The Pleasures of Love
William's Wife
Victoria Victorious

WHAT I SAW AND HOW I LIED • Judy Blundell
Evie's stepfather Joe returns from the War and takes them to a

rainy vacation on Palm Beach. Evie falls in love with the handsome ex-GI Peter who her father is not too fond of. Evie realizes that nothing is as it seems, and she will have to betray one of the three people she loves the most.

Other books by the author:
> Strings Attached
>
> Disappearing Act
>
> A City Tossed and Broken: The Diary of Minnie Bonner, San Francisco, California, 1906

FEVER 1793 • Laurie Halse Anderson

Matilda has big plans. She lives with her mother, grandfather and Eliza, a freed slave, in the apartment on top of their family coffeehouse in Philadelphia and wants to turn her coffeehouse into the finest business in Philadelphia. Then the yellow fever strikes, and people drop down dead or flee the once bustling city.

FLASH GOLD • Lindsay Buroker

First in the Flash Gold Chronicles, the novel is about eighteen-year-old Kali McAlister who has to survive the smugglers and other thugs who are seeking her out. They believe she has the recipe of Flash Gold, her alchemist father's greatest invention.

Other books in the Flash Gold series:
> Hunted
>
> Peacemaker

MEET THE AUTHOR
GEORGETTE HEYER

Heyer is best known for her historical romance novels set in the British Regency period among the wealthy upper class. Heyer researched meticulously before embarking on a book.

She had more than a thousand reference books and her library included histories of snuff boxes, sign posts and costumes. Her notes were sorted into categories such as Beauty, Colours, Dress, Hats, Household, Prices and Shops!

Heyer also wrote thrillers.

In *The Spanish Bride*, Brigade-Major Harry Smith dives headlong into marriage. In his beautiful child-bride, Juana, he finds a kindred spirit and a temper to match.

The Conqueror chronicles the life of William of Normandy. Born the illegitimate son of Robert, future Duke of Normandy, William has to fight to prove himself in the eyes of his people and his enemies.

Other books by the author:
Heyer wrote more than forty-eight books, some of which are:
- The Talisman Ring
- These Old Shades
- Devil's Club
- Regency Buck
- An Infamous Army
- Arabella
- The Grand Sophy
- Cotillion
- Bath Tangle
- Venetia
- Frederica

CLEOPATRA'S DAUGHTER • Michelle Moran

Selene and Alexander are the two children of Cleopatra and Anthony who survive the journey from Egypt to Rome when their parents kill themselves instead of surrendering to Octavian. In Rome, Octavia, the woman Anthony had left to be with Cleopatra,

is entrusted with bringing up the two orphans.
Other books by the author:
> Nefertiti
> The Heretic Queen
> Madame Tussaud: A Novel of the French Revolution
> The Second Empress

THE FAR PAVILIONS • M.M. Kaye

After the death of his parents, Ashton Pelham-Martyn is brought up as an Indian, Ashok. He meets and falls in love with Anjuli, a princess of mixed heritage like him. When he returns as an adult to India, his love for Anjuli is undiminished and together, they must survive the intrigues in her kingdom.
Other books by the author:
> Kaye wrote a number of novels, some of which are:
> Shadow of the Moon
> Trade Winds
> The Ordinary Princess

GONE WITH THE WIND • Margaret Mitchell

The epic love story of ruthless Scarlett O'Hara and Rhett Butler in the times of the American Civil War. It is a tale of beating the odds, of love and loss, and of a nation that changed forever.

A BRIEF HISTORY OF MONTMARAY • Michelle Cooper

It is 1936 and war is distant for the eccentric family in the island kingdom of Montmaray. Sophie receives a diary and records the happenings in her island. Everything changes when two men in a ship with a Swastika flag come to their island.
Other books in The Montmaray Journals series:
> The FitzOsbornes in Exile

The FitzOsbornes at War

STARCURSED • Nandini Bajpai
In the ancient city of Ujjayani, the planets align to decide the fate of two starcursed lovers. Born under the curse of Mars, brilliant and beautiful Leelavati, daughter of the famed astronomer Bhaskarya Acharya of Ujjayani, knows she can never wed. But when her childhood playmate, the handsome and rich Rahul Nagarseth, returns from sea, their attraction is rekindled under the stars.

BETSEY BROWN • Ntozake Shange
Betsey Brown is an African-American seventh-grader growing up in St. Louis, Missouri and is chosen to attend the white school in an attempt to end segregation at schools in the Civil Rights Movement in the US.

Other books by the author:
- Sassafrass, Cypress and Indigo
- Ellington was not a Street
- Some Sing, Some Cry

THE OTHER BOLEYN GIRL • Philippa Gregory
Mary Boleyn was the first Boleyn girl to catch Henry VIII's eye in his court. She is dazzled with him but then realizes that he is fascinated with her sister Anne. And Mary must pass on all her knowledge to Anne for the sake of her family's position at the court.

Other books in the Tudor series:
- The Queen's Fool
- The Virgin's Lover
- The Constant Princess

The Boleyn Inheritance
The Other Queen

GRAVE MERCY • R.L. LaFevers
Seventeen-year-old Ismae is no ordinary girl. When she escapes from an arranged marriage into the sanctuary of a convent, she realizes that she has dangerous gifts and a violent future. She is trained to become an assassin.
Other books in the His Fair Assassin series:
Dark Triumph
Mortal Heart

COPPER SUN • Sharon Draper
Amari leads a great life in Africa. She is engaged to the best man in her tribe and is among people who love her. She is captured and sent to the US as a slave and her life is torturous. She is entrusted to Polly for training and slowly, the two girls become best friends and decide to escape the cruel plantation owner.
Other books by the author:
Out of My Mind
Hazelwood High series

FLYGIRL • Sherri Smith
When the US enters the war with Germany and Japan, the Army creates WASP, the Women's Airforce Service Pilots. Ida has always wanted to fly. There is one hitch—black women are not allowed to apply, and Ida is black.
Other books by the author:
Hot, Sour, Salty, Sweet
Lucy the Giant
Sparrow

THE GRASSHOPPER'S RUN • Siddhartha Sarma
In 1944, the Japanese army invaded British India through the East. When the Japanese massacre a whole village, they kill Gojen's best friend Uti. Gojen wants to avenge his friend's death and travels to Kohima.

CASHELMARA • Susan Howatch
The widower Edward marries Marguerite, a young bright woman and gets her home to Cashelmara, his family home in Ireland. The young bride is caught up in secrets and intrigue at Cashelmara and her life becomes a nightmare.

Other books by the author:
 Penmarric
 The Starbridge Series

THE SWORD IN THE STONE • T.H. White
Wart grows up in the castle of his foster father Sir Ector and spends his time with Kay, Sir Ector's son and heir. Wart meets the magician Merlyn who spends the next six years teaching Wart to be a gentleman. When Kay is knighted, the Wart becomes his squire. Together the two travel to London for the tournament which will decide the next king of England.

Other books in the Once and Future King series:
 The Queen of Air and Darkness
 The Ill-Made Knight
 The Candle in the Wind
 The Book of Merlyn

RIVER IN THE SEA • Tina Boscha
Leen is a typical fifteen-year-old girl. She is carefree but she is also a little nervous about the German soldiers stationed nearby.

When a German soldier's dog runs in front of her truck, Leen's life is changed forever.

THE NAME OF THE ROSE • Umberto Eco

The year is 1327. Monks of the Benedictines order are mysteriously killed in the most bizarre fashion. In attendance is William of the Franciscan order who has come there to investigate heresy. Now William sets out to solve the murders.

Other books by the author:

Foucault's Pendulum
The Island of the Day Before
The Prague Cemetery

CHILD OF A DREAM • Valerio Massimo Manfredi

Even before he was born, the son of Philip of Macedonia and his wife Olympias was determined for greatness. Alexander is tutored by Aristotle and counts Ptolemy and Hephiaston as his close friends. Together with a band of loyal men, Alexander sets out to achieve glory.

Other books in the Alexandros series:

The Sands of Ammon
The Ends of Earth

YOUR HISTORICAL FICTION CHECKLIST

List down the books as you read them. Also rate them and share the ratings with your friends!

Rating scale

Absolutely Smashing—4
Very Good—3
Strictly OK—2
Did Not Like It One Bit—1

Read the Book	Rating

Humour

Full of humour—dark and light—these books will make you laugh at things you did not think possible.

LEVEL 1

MOIN AND THE MONSTER • Anushka Ravishankar

Young Moin hears a monster under his bed. The monster threatens Moin to draw him else he will be turned into a suitcase. The problem is, Moin is not good at drawing. So the monster comes alive looking pink, with drumstick legs and autorickshaw horns. Now Moin is stuck with him—forever.

Other books by the author:
- Moin and the Monster Songster
- The Elephant Never Forgets
- Tiger on a Tree
- The Rumour
- To Market, To Market

TEEN BOAT! • Dave Roman, John Green

Teen Boat is just that—a teenager who turns into a boat if he gets any liquid in his ears. He wants to create an identity for himself in school—with disastrous results.

Other books by the author:
- The Astronaut Academy series

A HANDFUL OF HORRID HENRY • Francesca Simon
An incorrigible boy who is always in trouble, whether with the tooth fairy or his teacher at school. And his life is not any easier because his brother happens to be Perfect Peter.

Other Horrid Henry books:
There are a number of Horrid Henry books, some of which are:
- Horrid Henry Gets Rich Quick
- Horrid Henry's Haunted House
- Horrid Henry's Nits
- Horrid Henry's Stink Bomb
- Horrid Henry and the Mummy's Curse
- Horrid Henry's Underpants

MEET THE AUTHOR
ROALD DAHL

Roald Dahl was a British novelist, short story writer, poet, fighter pilot and a screenwriter. He is considered to be 'one of the world's greatest storytellers for children of the twentieth century'. His stories were very different from others of the time–they came with dark humour and unexpected ends.

The Twits is about an elderly couple who spend their lives playing nasty tricks on each other. They also enjoy being cruel to animals and hate children. The arrival of the Roly Poly Bird from Africa allows the victims to get sweet revenge.

Charlie and the Chocolate Factory is about a boy named Charlie Bucket who lives in extreme poverty with his extended family. Charlie finds a rare golden ticket in his chocolate bar and is permitted to enter Willy Wonka's magical candy factory.

Other books by Roald Dahl:
- James and the Giant Peach
- Matilda

The Witches
Fantastic Mr Fox
George's Marvellous Medicine
The BFG
The Wonderful World of Henry Sugar
Revolting Rhymes
Dirty Beasts

DIARY OF A WIMPY KID • Jeff Kinney

Greg gets into middle school and his mom forces him to keep a diary. And if he has to find his groove in school, it is no easy work at home either with an attention-seeking younger brother Manny and an evil older brother Rodrick.

Other books in the Diary of a Wimpy Kid series:
Rodrick Rules
The Last Straw
Dog Days
The Ugly Truth
Cabin Fever
The Third Wheel

FUNNY BUSINESS • Jon Scieszka and various authors

Ten hilarious stories for boys—from a homicidal turkey to the only boy in class who does not have a super power to turn into a vampire or a superhero, this anthology has been put together by some of the best children's authors.

Other books in the Guys Read Library of Great Reading series:
Thriller
The Sports Pages

TIK-TIK, THE MASTER OF TIME • Musharraf Ali Farooqi

On the planet Nopter, somewhere deep in the cosmos, young Tik-Tik has a BIG problem. He wants to grow faster than or at least as fast as his furry enemy, Dum-Dum the cat. So Tik-Tik sets off with his Grandpa Kip-Kip on an adventure to find a solution to his problem. They land up on a growing planet called Earth.
Other books by the author:
> The Amazing Moustaches of Moochchander the Iron Man and Other Stories
> Rabbit Rap

WISHA WOZZARITER • Payal Kapadia

Ten-year-old Wisha wishes to be a writer. When she meets Bookworm, she stops wishing and starts writing. With him, she rides on the Thought Express to the Marketplace of Ideas, the Superhero Salon and the Bargain Bazaar, and encounters a motley crew of characters. Along the way, she discovers the creative process by which anything beautiful and lasting is created.

BOTTERSNIKES AND GUMBLES • S.A. Wakefield

The Bottersnikes are fat, selfish and endlessly lazy heaps. They want to catch Gumbles, put them in jam jars and make them work for them. Gumbles are small, but smart…

WHERE THE SIDEWALK ENDS • Shel Silverstein

Where the sidewalk ends, Shel Silverstein's world begins. This collection of poems is beautifully illustrated. Meet a child who has a life-threatening disease till he realizes that it is a holiday and a little boy and an old man who are in a similar predicament.
Other books by the author:

A Light in the Attic
Falling Up
Lafcadio, The Lion Who Shot Back

LEVEL 2

CALVIN AND HOBBES • Bill Waterson
A precocious six-year-old Calvin and his stuffed tiger Hobbes (who comes alive when alone with Calvin) are the heroes of this delightful series. Calvin has an opinion on everything and is in a constant conflict with Susan, his classmate.
There are a number of books, some of which are:
The Days Are Just Packed
Something Under the Bed Is Drooling
Yukon Ho!
Weirdos from Another Planet
The Revenge of the Baby-Sat
There's Treasure Everywhere

NO MORE DEAD DOGS • Gordon Korman
Wallace Wallace gets into trouble at middle school for telling the truth. He hated the book *Old Shep, My Pal* and writes a scathing review on it. The English teacher Mr Fogelman is not amused. Wallace gets detention, is forced to miss football and has to sit through the school's preparations for dramatizing *Old Shep, My Pal*. Finally Wallace changes the play completely.
Other books by the author:
Swindle series
On the Run series
Island series
Macdonald Hall series

LOVE AMONG THE WALNUTS • Jean Ferris

Horatio and his wife Mousey are happily married and live in a country estate with their millions and their son Sandy and valet Bentley. Sandy's greedy uncles poisons a birthday cake that puts the couple in a coma. Can Sandy and Bentley revive the couple or will the greedy uncles get all the wealth?

Other books by the author:
   Upon a Marigold series
   Of Sound Mind
   Much Ado about Grubstake

OUT FROM BONEVILLE • Jeff Smith

Phoney Bone has to leave town because of his dubious deals and his cousins Fone and Smiley go along with him. Soon the three Bones are separated and lost in the desert. Phoney comes to a lush valley and wants to look for his cousins. The only problem is that the giant rats in the valley think Phoney would make for a tasty treat.

Others books in the Bone series:
   The Great Cow Race
   Eyes of the Storm
   The Dragon Slayers
   Rock Jaw: Master of the Eastern Border
   Old Man's Cave
   Ghost Circles
   Treasure Hunters
   Crown of Horns

MEET THE AUTHOR
P.G. WODEHOUSE

Sir Pelham Grenville Wodehouse enjoyed enormous popular success during a career that lasted more than seventy years. His body of work includes novels, short stories, plays, poems and song lyrics.

He is best known for the Jeeves and Blandings Castle novels and short stories.

Something Fresh is the first novel set in Blandings Castle. Ashe Marson and Joan Valentine land up at Blandings for some time out as well as to retrieve a scarab. They have no idea what a scarab is, except for the fact that it belongs to an American millionaire and has been unintentionally stolen by the forgetful Lord Emsworth.

Other books by P.G. Wodehouse:
- Blandings
- Heavy Weather
- Blandings Castle and Elsewhere
- Lord Emsworth and Others
- Full Moon
- Pigs Have Wings
- Galahad at Blandings
- A Pelican at Blandings
- Sunset at Blandings
- Jeeves and Wooster
- The Inimitable Jeeves
- Carry On, Jeeves
- Right Ho, Jeeves
- Thank You, Jeeves
- The Code of the Woosters
- The Mating Season

Jeeves and the Feudal Spirit
Stiff Upper Lip, Jeeves
Much Obliged, Jeeves
Aunts aren't Gentlemen

THE SECRET BLOG OF RAISIN RODRIGUEZ • Judy Goldschmidt

TwoScoopsofRaisin.com, is the blog of Raisin Rodriguez. She has moved to a new town, is having adjustment problems and misses her two best friends Pia and Claudia.

Other books in the Raisin Rodrigues series:
> Raisin Rodriguez and the Big-Time Smooch
> Will the Real Raisin Rodriguez Please Stand Up?

ALL-AMERICAN GIRL • Meg Cabot

Samantha Madison is an average, cool teen. Her life changes suddenly when she saves the President of the United States from an assassination attempt. Now apart from the other things this reluctant teen celebrity has to cope with, there is also David, the President's son, who she likes a lot.

Other books in the All American Girl series:
> Ready or Not

Other books by the author:
> The Mediator
> Boy X
> Queen of Babble
> Heather Wells
> The Princess Diaries

GOOPY GYNE, BAGHA BYNE • Upendrakishore Ray Chowdhury

Goopy wants to be a singer and knows only one song. Bagha wants to be a musician and can drum only one rhythm on the drums. They both meet in the jungle where they have been sent by their village folk, who cannot listen to them anymore.

LEVEL 3

THE DOWNSIDE OF BEING UP • Alan Lawrence Sitomer

Bobby Connor is not having the easiest time. His family is nuts, his sister hates him and he cannot get any girl to like him. And then he does something that lands the maths teacher in the hospital.
Other books by the author:
>   Homeboyz
>   Hip-Hop High School
>   The Hoopster
>   Daddies Do it Different

THE BOOK OF BUNNY SUICIDES • Andy Riley

When rabbits think they have had enough of the world, they start committing suicide. But there are many many ways of dying. For instance, two bunnies refuse to board Noah's Ark and instead they read a book, have a drink and sunbathe till death comes calling.
Other books by the author:
>   Return of the Bunny Suicides
>   Great Lies to Tell Small Kids

HOW TO SURVIVE A ROBOT UPRISING • Daniel H. Wilson

What would you do if robots turned against you? And how would you know if the robots were turning against you? Simple—they stop doing the work they were designed for and start doing something else.

KING DORK • Frank Portman

Outcast Tom is not having a great time in high school. He is sorting out issues over his father's death, aiming to form a band with his one best friend, and also trying to find the mystery girl he had met at a party.

ME AND EARL AND THE DYING GIRL • Jesse Andrews

Greg and his friend Earl share a love for movies and shoot their own incomprehensible versions of Coppola and Herzog classics. Greg's mother forces him to rekindle his friendship with Rachel who is suffering from leukemia. And Rachel finds out about the movies.

MEET THE AUTHOR
THE HARVARD LAMPOON

Published since 1876, *The Harvard Lampoon* is the world's longest, continually published humour magazine. The organisation also produces occasional parodies of bestsellers.

Bored of the Rings is a parody of *The Lord of the Rings*, by J.R.R. Tolkein. The parody follows the style of the original book, with the preface, prologue, poetry and songs. Gandalf Greyhame becomes Goodgulf Greyteeth and Hobbits are Boggies!

The Hunger Pains is a parody of *The Hunger Games*, by

Suzanne Collins. When Kantkiss Neverclean replaces her sister as a contestant in 'The Hunger Games'—the second-highest rated reality show in Peaceland, right after 'Extreme Home Makeover'—she has no idea what to expect!

Nightlight is a parody of Stephanie Meyer's *Twilight*. Pale and klutzy Belle arrives in Switchblade, Oregon and discovers Edwart, a super-hot computer nerd with zero interest in girls. She discovers he is a vampire. But how can Belle convince Edwart to bite her and transform her into his eternal bride, especially when he seems to find girls so repulsive?

THWONK • Joan Bauer

Sometimes having your dream come true is not really pleasant. When A.J. meets cupid Jonathan, she asks for Peter Terris to fall in love with her. A.J. realizes her mistake soon enough as she has nothing in common with Peter and Jonathan seems to have disappeared.

Other books by the author:
- Hope Was Here
- Close to Famous
- Rules of the Road series
- Peeled

PSYCH INVESTIGATION EPISODES: EPISODE 1 • Kevin Weinberg

Jack Harris cares only about popcorn and television. Then he discovers he has superpowers—the kind that set his classroom on fire. Jack becomes a suspect in some gruesome murders, and also has a group of murderers chasing him to join them.

I LOVE YOU, BETH COOPER • Larry Doyle
The nerd and valedictorian Denis Cooverman didn't want to give a typical graduation speech so he stood up in front of all his classmates and their three thousand relatives and said something really important—'I love you, Beth Cooper.' Beth's boyfriend is not amused.
Other books by the author:
> Go, Mutants!
> Deliriously Happy: and Other Bad Thoughts

A FATE TOTALLY WORSE THAN DEATH • Paul Fleischman
Danielle and her two friends are a cruel bunch. The kind who won't give an old woman a seat on the bus or eat up the chocolates of inmates during community service. When Helga from Norway comes as an exchange student to their school, the girls get jealous and plan to trouble Helga. Little do they know what's coming their way.
Other books by the author:
> The Dunderheads
> Bull Run
> The Matchbox Diary
> The Borning Room

LIES, KNIVES AND GIRLS IN RED DRESSES • Ron Koertge
Retellings of some of the popular fairy tales, this has the Beast getting bored and missing his fangs, of Cinderella's sisters having surgery and Red Riding Hood trying to tell her mother the story. Written in free verse, these twenty stories are an absolute blast.
Other books by the author:

Shakespeare Bats Cleanup series
Stoner and Spaz series
Boy Girl Boy

WORDYGURDYBOOM! ABOL TABOL: THE NONSENSE WORLD OF SUKUMAR RAY • Sukumar Ray

A selection of poems from the Bengali classics *Abol Tabol* and *Khai-Khai* among other things there are a kingdom where the queen wears a pillow on her head and the king howls like a fox.

YOUR HUMOUR CHECKLIST

List down the books as you read them. Also rate them and share the ratings with your friends!

Rating scale

Absolutely Smashing—4
Very Good—3
Strictly OK—2
Did Not Like It One Bit—1

Read the Book	Rating

Manga Comics

All age groups in Japan read Manga. Manga comics cover most genres—adventure, crime, romance, mystery—and follow a style developed in the late nineteenth century in Japan. Most manga stories are printed in black and white and are usually read from back to front. A manga artist is called a mangaka. The following titles can be enjoyed by all age groups.

NANA • Ai Yazawa
Two twenty-year-old women share the same name: Nana. They meet on the train and go on to become flatmates and best friends and discover a world of music, fashion, parties and gossip.

PARADISE KISS • Ai Yazawa
School is Yukari's life and she has a condescending attitude towards the fashion students. She is kidnapped one afternoon by 'Paradise Kiss', a group of fashion students. She begins to respect and admire them, and also falls for George, the group's leader.

FULL MOON O SAGASHITE • Arina Tanemura
Mitsuki loves to sing, but the operation that can cure her of her sarcoma can also destroy her vocal cords. She is helped by two magical beings and becomes a healthy sixteen-year-old. However, she has only a year to live. She has to make her name in the musical world, and also hope that her love Eichi who is far away

from her will hear her sing and understand her love for him.

OURAN HIGH SCHOOL HOST CLUB • Bisco Hatori
Haruhi, a scholarship student is seeking peace and quiet and stumbles upon a private place where the Ouran High School's rich kids entertain their female friends. She breaks a $80,000 vase and is forced to work as a Host in the club, because the rich boys think she is a boy too.

TSUBASA: RESERVOIR CHRONICLE • Clamp
Sakura loses her soul and her childhood friend Syaoran goes on a quest to find it. He has to collect her memories that exist in alternate universes as feathers because that will help save her soul.

CHOBITS • Clamp
Chi lives in an alternate universe and isn't your average humanoid computer. Hideki finds her abandoned in the trash possibly because she could not perform any of the functions of computers. But together Hideki and Chi set out to explore the mysteries of Chi's origins.

XXX HOLIC • Clamp
Watanuki Kimihiro is haunted by visions of ghosts and spirits and wants them removed. He meets Yuuko who runs a small wish-granting shop. She removes this ability, but Kimihiro has to deal with other supernatural encounters now.

CARDCAPTOR SAKURA • Clamp
Sakura finds an enchanted book called *The Clow* in her father's library. She accidentally frees the set of magical cards in that. Now she must find all the cards before a catastrophe falls on the world.

ONE PIECE • Eiichiro Oda
Monkey Duffy wants to be the next Pirate King. He gains the properties of rubber after eating a devil's fruit. Together with his motley crew called the Straw Hat Pirates, Monkey Duffy sets out to achieve One Piece.

MARS • Fuyumi Soryo
Popular Rei and shy Kira are worlds apart, but become attracted to each other. They both have dark secrets, and help each other cope with the pain.

THE BUG BOY • Hideshi Hino
This is part of the Hino Horror series. Sanpei is a young lonely boy who is constantly victimized. He is bitten by a bug and soon his body begins to decompose and he becomes a caterpillar-like insect. Rejected by his family too, Sanpei leaves home and takes his revenge on all the people who troubled him in the past.

HANA-KIMI • Hisaya Nakajo
Japanese-American Mizuki is a star athlete and in love with high jumper Izumi Sano. She manages to transfer to his school. There is a catch however—Sano goes to an all-boys school and Mizuki has to disguise herself.

MAID SAMA! • Hiro Fujiwara
Misaki is a beacon in the Seika High School which was till recently an all-boys' school and where girls still feel a bit out of place. Misaki is revered and feared in school, but is having an uncomfortable time, since the popular boy Takumi sees her in a maid's uniform post school and begins to take an interest in her.

FULLMETAL ALCHEMIST • Hiromu Arakawa
Two brothers Edward and Alphonse Eric are seeking the Philsopher's Stone to regain limbs and the strength of their bodies. Their earlier attempt to harness the power of alchemy resulted in the death of their mother and had disastrous consequences for them.

BLACK BIRD • Kanoko Sakurakouji
Misao Harada can see magical beings but she only wants to live a normal life. Then one day she is attacked by a demon, and Kyo comes to save her. Kyo is not the boy you would want as your boyfriend.

HIGH SCHOOL DEBUT • Kazune Kawahara
Haruna has a new plan for high school—she wants to get a boyfriend and fall in love. Since she does not have the requisite skills to get a boyfriend, she enlists the help of the popular Yoh. He agrees on only one condition: she must not fall in love with him.

NARUTO • Masashi Kishimoto
Teen ninja-in-training, Naruto Uzumaki wants to become a Hokage, the greatest ninja in the land but his grades at the Ninja Academy are poor and most adults shun this orphan boy.

PET SHOP OF HORRORS SERIES • Matsuri Akino
Detective Leon suspects that Count D uses his pet shop as a front for drug trafficking. Count D has rare animals with humanoid features and each comes with a contract that must be adhered to, else it results in a disaster for the buyer.

VAMPIRE KNIGHT • Matsuri Hino
Yuki has only one memory of her childhood. At ten, she was attacked by a vampire and saved by another. What is the connection between Kaname, who Yuki loves, and her? And what of her friend Zero Kiryu who hates vampires?

SAILOR MOON • Naoko Takeuchi
Usagi Tsukino is no ordinary girl. She is a Sailor Moon, the bunch of girls who fight the evils in the universe. Each girl transforms into a warrior named after a planet or the Moon. With other Sailor Senshi she fights the forces of evil.

FRUITS BASKET • Natsuki Takaya
Tohru loses her mother and finds an unlikely home with her rich classmate Yuki and his family. She realizes that her friend and his family, the Sohmas, have a secret. They are inhabited by the spirits of the twelve zodiac signs and change into their zodiac animal when hugged by the opposite sex. She sets out to break the curse.

RUROUNI KENSHIN • Nobuhiro Watsuki
Himura was an infamous assassin in the early Meji era. Now he roams the countryside providing protection to anyone who needs it in an attempt to atone for his sins.

BLEACH • Tite Kubo
Ichigo Kurosaki becomes a Soul Reaper, protecting humans from evil spirits and ensuring that the departed sould get a safe passage to the other world. His powers have come to him from Rukia, and now her superiors want to punish her.

DEATH NOTE • Tsugumi Ohba
Light Yagami's life changes when he finds a notebook called the Death Note. Any human whose name appears in the notebook dies. Light decides to use this power to rid the world of evil. Will he succeed?

BLACK BUTLER • Yana Toboso
Sebastian is the butler of the enormously successful Phantomhive heir, the young Earl Phantomhive. He is there to help the earl in all his chores, including avenging his parents' death. In return, Sebastian can consume Earl's soul when all the tasks are over.

SKIP BEAT! • Yoshiki Nakamura
Kyoko has forever loved Sho and supported his musician ambitions. She is heartbroken when Sho confesses he was only using her. Kyoko vows to take revenge.

D.N. ANGEL • Yukiru Sugisaki
Daisuke has a strange genetic condition and transforms into phantom thief Dark whenever he thinks too much about his crush on Risa. Daisuke is friendly with the commander of police whose alter-ego Krad dislikes Dark. Daisuke can be cured only when his unrequited love is returned.

ABSOLUTE BOYFRIEND • Yuu Watase
When Riizo Izawa creates the perfect boyfriend on a website, little does she know that he will be delivered to her doorstep one morning. She falls in love with him, but Night was hers only for 72 hours, and she must shell out a large sum of money if she wants to retain him.

YOUR MANGA CHECKLIST

List down the books as you read them. Also rate them and share the ratings with your friends!

Rating scale

    Absolutely Smashing—4
    Very Good—3
    Strictly OK—2
    Did Not Like It One Bit—1

Read the Book	Rating

Science Fiction

Superior technology, space travel, aliens, paranormal qualities and maybe a dystopian world too, science fiction is always fun to read.

LEVEL 1

RITE OF PASSAGE • Alexei Panshin
In 2140 AD, Earth has been destroyed and the survivors live on seven giant starships. Mia, the daughter of the Chairman of the Ship's Council, must go through a month of trial in the hostile wilds of a colony world. Mia decides to use the tiger strategy and fight for her survival in the colony, instead of being a turtle and hiding out the month.

Other books by the author:
>Star Well
>The Thurb Revolution
>Masque World
>Heinlein in Dimension
>Farewell to Yesterday's Tomorrow

DRAGONSONG • Ann McCaffrey
Menolly is a gifted musician but her talent is scorned upon in her world of Pern. She escapes and discovers the legendary fire-wizards that are Pern's first line of defence. Menolly goes on to become

the first female Harper, and also realizes her musical dreams. Other books in the Harper Hall trilogy:

    Dragonslayer
    Dragondrums

MY TEACHER IS AN ALIEN • Bruce Coville

The new substitute teacher at school is really an alien—an orange-eyed, green humanoid called Broxholm with evil designs on Earth. Susan and her friends Peter and Duncan must save the world.
Other books in the My Teacher is an Alien series:

    My Teacher Fried My Brains
    My Teacher Glows in the Dark
    My Teacher Flunked the Planet

ALAN MENDELSOHN, THE BOY FROM MARS • Daniel Pinkwater

Leonard and his friend Alan, who claims he is a Martian, meet Samuel Klugarsh, the owner of an occult store. They travel to Waka-Waka, a lost civilization.
Other books by the author:

    Slaves of Spiegel
    The Snarkout Boys and the Avocado of Death
    The Last Guru

THE CITY OF EMBER • Jeanne DuPrau

Lina and Doon live in an underground city which is on the verge of collapsing. They must find the box and decode the messages that can help save the city.
Others in the Book of Ember series:

    The People of Sparks
    The Prophet of Yonwood
    The Diamond of Darkhold

THE WHITE MOUNTAINS • John Christopher

The Capping Day is an important ritual for children making the transition to adulthood in a future Earth. Tripod, the three-legged machines, rule the earth with 'capped' human beings, Before his capping day, thirteen-year-old Will meets a Vagrant, and sets out to look for a world beyond the control of the Tripods.

Others in the Tripods series:
- The City of Gold and Lead
- The Pool of Fire
- When the Tripods Came

MEET THE AUTHOR
JULES VERNE

Jules Verne was the pioneer of this genre. He wrote about space, air and underwater travels.

In *A Journey to the Centre of the Earth*, a German professor believes there are volcanic tubes going toward the centre of the Earth. He takes his nephew Axel and a guide and they all descend into an extinct Icelandic volcano. They come to surface in southern Italy after numerous adventures.

Some of Jules Verne's other books are:
- The Adventures of Captain Hatteras
- The Lighthouse at the End of the World
- In Search of the Castaway
- The Mysterious Island
- Twenty Thousand Leagues Under the Sea
- Around the World in 80 Days
- From the Earth to the Moon

RUNNING OUT OF TIME • Margaret Peterson Haddix

Jessie lives with her family in the frontier village of Clifton,

Indiana. She thinks she is in the 1840s. Diptheria strikes the village, and her mother reveals to her that this is actually 1996. Jessie must get out of the village to get help, but it is not easy to get out of the heavily guarded village.

THE EAR, THE EYE AND THE ARM • Nancy Farmer

Zimbabwe in 2194 AD. General Matsika is waging a war against many tribes and locks his children in a fortified mansion for their safety. The bored children escape and the General must enlist the help of the Ear, the Eye and the Arm to get them back safe.
Other books by the author:
   Sea of Trolls series
   The House of the Scorpion
   A Girl Named Disaster
   The Warm Place

ONLY YOU CAN SAVE MANKIND • Terry Pratchett

Johnny Maxwell plays a pirated version of the new game *Only You Can Save Mankind*. The ScreeWee Empire surrenders to him without putting up too much fight, and the empire seems to have disappeared from other people's games. What is going on?
Other books in the Johnny Maxwell series:
   Johnny and the Dead
   Johnny and the Bomb

LEVEL 2

THE STARS ARE OURS! • Andre Norton

Knowledge is spurned in this future world and scientists are a maligned lot who have gone into hiding. Las Nordis, one such scientist, makes his son Dard memorize a series of numbers.

When Lars is killed, Dard and his sister escape to find the other scientists. But what of the numbers that Dard has memorized?
Other books in the Astra series:
> Star Born

Other books by the author:
> Halfblood Chronicles
> Witch World series

EMERGENCE • David Palmer
Candy writes in her diary while living in a bomb shelter, waiting for the effects of a bio-nuclear war to pass. She emerges to find that very few of her species survived and she sets out to find other post-war survivors.
Other books by the author:
> Threshold
> Tracking
> George Washington's Military Genius

DAVY • Edgar Pangborn
A post apocalyptic US has deteriorated into many squabbling states. The Holy Murcan Church is the dominant power and discourages learning. It also dictates that Mues, the mutants, be killed. Davy is taken away from his mother and is on the run.
Other books by the author:
> A Mirror for Observers
> Still I Persist in Wondering
> West of the Sun
> The Company of Glory
> The Judgement of Eve

LITTLE FUZZY • H. Beam Piper

A company manages the planet Zararthustra and has the exclusive rights on new discoveries there. One day, a small furry creature is discovered. Are these intelligent creatures sapient? If yes, then the planet will be declared protected, and the company will lose all exclusive rights there.

Other Fuzzy books:
> Fuzzy Sapiens
> Fuzzies and Other People

Other books by the author:
> Lord Kalvan of Otherwhen

THE MAZE RUNNER • James Dashner

Thomas and a bunch of kids are inside a maze. No one has any memory of the past or how they got into the maze. Getting out of the maze is impossible—the grievers are machines that can sting you or kill you. And if stung, you may be able to remember some past memories.

Other books in the Maze Runner series:
> The Kill Order
> Thomas's First Memory of the Flare
> The Scorch Trials
> The Death Cure

ORBITAL RESONANCE • John Barnes

Melpomene Murray lives on the Flying Dutchman asteroid somewhere between an Earth destroyed by disease and war and Mars. She discovers that she is being manipulated—but she does not mind it. Rather she quites enjoys it.

Other books in The Century Next Door series:
> Kaleidoscope

Candle
The Sky So Big and Black

CINDER • Marissa Meyer
Cinder is a cyborg and must guard her secret. Her father is dead and she is blamed for his death by her stepmother and stepsisters. The ruthless lunar people are watching from space and the fate of Earth hinges on her.

Other books in the Lunar Chronicles series:
Glitches
Scarlet
Cress
Winter

THE HOUSE OF THE SCORPION • Nancy Farmer
Matteo Alacran is a clone—he was harvested from the DNA from El Patron, lord of a country called Opium. He exists with the sole purpose of giving his organs to El Patron when his organs fail him. But is that really his destiny?

Other books in the Matteo Alacran series:
The Lord of Opium

Other books by the author:
The Sea of Trolls series
The Ear, the Eye and the Arm
A Girl Named Disaster
The Warm Place

UNWIND • Neal Shusterman
The Second Civil War was fought over reproductive rights. Now according to the compromise reached, parents will have to sign over their children past thirteen years for organ harvesting. Three

children question this.
Other books in the Unwind series:
> UnStrung
> UnWholly
> UnBroken

EARTHSEED • Pamela Sargent
A ship carries in it the seed of humankind in the shape of Zoheret and her mates. Now the children must leave the safety of the ship and learn to live in an uninhabited planet...
Other books in The Seed series:
> Farseed
> Seed Seeker

SHIP BREAKER • Paulo Bacigalupi
Nailer works as a ship breaker in a future world where rising sea levels have destroyed governments and created new power structures. Nailer wants freedom and one day, he and his friend Pima find a ship that will help them buy their freedom.
Other books in the Ship Breaker series:
> The Drowned Cities

EVA • Peter Dickinson
Thirteen-year-old Eva is critically injured and the only way to save her is to transplant her brain into the body of a chimp. Will she be happy?
Other books by the author:
> The Changes trilogy
> The Gift
> The Blue-Hawk
> Annerton Pit

I AM NUMBER FOUR • Pittacus Lore

Nine Gardes from a planet called Lorein escaped to Earth when the evil Mogadorians destroyed it. They were to live amongst earthlings and grow strong to return to free Lorein. But one by one the Gardes begin to be killed. Will Number Four survive?

Other books in the Lorein Legacies series:

The Power of Six
The Rise of Nine

MEET THE AUTHOR
H.G. WELLS

Along with Jules Verne, Wells is sometimes referred to as the 'Father of Science Fiction'. He was a prolific writer and wrote more than a hundred books of fiction and non-fiction.

The Invisible Man is the story of a brilliant scientist Griffin who creates a serum to render himself invisible.

In *The Time Machine* a time traveller is propelled into the future, to the year 802,701 AD where he meets peaceful humanoids called Eloi. His time machine is stolen by the strange ape-like creatures called Morlocks.

Other books by the author:

The Invisible Man
The War of the Worlds
The First Men in the Moon
When the Sleeper Wakes

THE GIRL OF FIRE AND THORNS • Rae Carson

Elisa is the chosen one who will do great things for mankind. When she is sixteen, she is married off to a handsome king, whose kingdom is under threat. When she is whisked away by an unlikely captor, she begins to see where her destiny lies.

Other books in the Fire and Thorns series:
- The Shadow Cats
- The Shattered Mountain
- The King's Guard
- The Crown of Embers
- The Bitter Kingdom

TUNNEL IN THE SKY • Robert Heinlein

Rod Walker is a student in Dr Matson's Advanced Survival class. In the final exam of the course, the students are sent into the wilderness to cope with nature until they are picked up at a specified time. But something is wrong—the pick-up date comes and goes and Rod and his classmates are not sure when they will be picked up, ever.

Other books by the author:
- Starship Troopers
- Have Space Suit, Will travel
- The Puppet Masters
- Podkayne of Mars

UGLIES • Scott Westerfeld

At sixteen, children undergo an operation that transforms them into very good looking people. Tally is waiting to become Pretty when her friend Shay runs away. Tally is faced with a tough choice—she must find Shay and turn her into the authorities, else she will never become Pretty.

Other books in the Uglies series:
- Pretties
- Specials
- Extras

THE HOST • Stephanie Meyer

The Earth has been invaded by an unseen enemy who take over the minds of the humans and leave their bodies intact. Wanderer takes over Melanie's body but is having a rough time because Melanie refuses to let go.

Other books by the author:
> The Twilight series

LIFE AS WE KNEW IT • Susan Beth Pfeffer

Miranda's world changes when an unexpected meteor pushes the moon closer to earth. There are tsunamis, gas and food rationing and the family struggles to keep their faith and hope alive.

Other books in the Last Survivors series:
> The Dead and the Gone
> This World We Live In

THE HUNGER GAMES • Suzanne Collins

Katniss Everdeen volunteers to take her sister's place in the annual Hunger Games contest. In the contest a boy and a girl from each of the twelve districts of Panem participate in a brutal reality show where only one child survives.

Other books in The Hunger Games trilogy:
> Catching Fire
> Mockingjay

A WIZARD OF EARTHSEA • Ursula K. Le Guin

Duny is a young boy who is willful and stubborn, but possesses a gift. He saves his village from Kargish invaders by a simple trick and this brings Ogion the Silent to him. Ogion gives him the name Ged and wants to teach him magic, as well as other qualities that a magician must possess to keep the balance of the

world. But Ged is impatient.
Other books in The Earthsea Cycle:
- The Tombs of Atuan
- The Farthest Shore
- Tehanu
- Tales from Earthsea
- The Other Wind

Other books by the author:
- The Lathe of Heaven
- The Dispossessed: An Ambiguous Utopia

DIVERGENT • Veronica Roth

On Choosing Day young Beatrice chooses the Dauntless faction instead of Abnegation, the one her family belongs to. Her brother Caleb chooses Erudite. But does Beatrice really fit in here, or is she a Divergent?

Other books in the Divergent series:
- Free Four: Tobias Tells the Story
- Insurgent

LEVEL 3

CHILDHOOD'S END • Arthur C. Clarke

Giant spaceships deliver the Overlords to Earth and they bring with them an era of peace, prosperity and health. The Overlords reveal their sinister plans after fifty years—they mean to eliminate humans.

Other books by the author:
- Space Odyssey series
- Rama series
- The Fountains of Paradise

ACROSS THE UNIVERSE • Beth Revis

Amy wakes up from her cryogenically induced sleep in 250 years—a good fifty years before she is scheduled to do so. She is aboard the spaceship Godspeed where Eldest has taken control and everyone does his bidding. Amy and Elder, the future leader of the ship, try to unravel the secrets.

Other books in the Across the Universe series:
- As They Slip Away
- A Million Suns
- Shades of Earth

LITTLE BROTHER • Cory Doctorow

Seventeen-year-old Marcus is smart in the networked world and can break through the clumsy surveillance systems of his high school. But he and his friends get into trouble when they are caught in the midst of a devastating terrorist attack. San Francisco becomes a police state, and when Marcus returns from detention and interrogation, he decides to fight back.

Other books by the author:
- For the Win
- A Place So Foreign and Eight More

GLORY SEASON • David Brin

As a half caste 'var', young Maia and her twin sister Leie must leave their home and seek their fortune in the world. The sisters are separated on two different ships and in a naval battle, Leie is lost at sea. Maia must survive alone.

Other books by the author:
- The Practice Effect
- The Postman
- Kiln People

THE SKYLARK OF SPACE • E.E. 'Doc' Smith
Dr Seaton is brilliant and handsome and engaged to the beautiful Dorothy. Yet, his mind is obsessed with the discovery of a metal that converts copper into pure energy. Only two other people believe him, his friend Crane who will help him, and Marc who sets out to destroy him.

Other books in the Skylark series:
    Skylark Three
    Skylark of Valeron
    Skylark DuQuesne
Other books by the author:
    The Lensman Series

DUNE • Frank Herbert
Melange is an important spice for humanity 21,000 years in the future. It facilitates mental abilities, health and extends life. Young Paul Atreides, the heir apparent of one of the Great Houses accepts the control of Arrakis, the desert planet that is the only source of melange.

Other books in the Dune series:
    Dune Messiah
    Children of the Dune
    God Emperor of Dune
    Heretics of Dune
    Chapterhouse: Dune

SHADE'S CHILDREN • Garth Nix
At fourteen, in a brutal city of the future, children are carted off to their death. They become machines that fight the battles to keep the evil Overlords in power. Some children have special talents, and Shade, a computer-generated simulation of an Adult

recruits them to fight the battle against the Overlords.
Other books by the author:
> The Abhorsen series
> The Keys to the Kingdom series

EARTH ABIDES • George Stewart

Ish survives a lethal plague and becomes the Last American to a new generation and his old hammer is the symbol of his power. He tries to preserve the knowledge of the days gone by, but then realizes that the new generation must be taught basic survival skills and tools like the bow and arrow.
Other books by the author:
> Storm
> Pickett's Charge
> Fire

AGAINST INFINITY • Gregory Benford

On the poisonous, icy surface of Ganymede roams an ancient artefact, the Aleph. The Aleph is made of stone and cuts through ice and mountains and destroys everything in its path. Can Manuel kill this monster?
Other books by the author:
> The Jupiter Project
> Timescape
> Foundation Fear
> The Galactic Center series

MISSION OF GRAVITY • Hal Clement

Planet Mesklin is a disc-shaped world with intense gravity. The intelligent creatures that live there are hydrogen breathing and caterpillar-like. When humans come exploring this planet,

Barlennan, a Mesklinite agrees to help them in return for rewards and profit.

Other books in the Mesklin series:
> Close to Critical
> Starlight

THE STAINLESS STEEL RAT • Harry Harrison

The Stainless Steel Rat is a slippery criminal. He is a master of disguises and a terrific liar. He is conned into joining the Special Corps, headed by a former crook, and has a series of adventures—including meeting and falling in love with Angelina, a fellow member of the Special Corps.

Other books in The Stainless Steel Rat series:
There are twelve books in the series, some of which are:
> The Stainless Steel Rat's Revenge
> The Stainless Steel Rat Saves the World
> The Stainless Steel Rat Wants You
> The Stainless Steel Rat for President

THE COMPLETE ROBOT • Isaac Asimov

There are three laws that robotics must follow: A robot may not injure a human being; a robot must obey the orders given by a human being (except where Law 1 kicks in) and a robot must protect his own existence (without violating Laws 1 and 2). In reality, this ethical system may not work.

Other books in The Complete Robot series:
> The Caves of Steel
> The Naked Sun
> The Robots of Dawn
> Robots and Empire

OLD MAN'S WAR • John Scalzi

In a futuristic world, men at the age of seventy-five are recruited into the army and given youth through a life-extending process. These 'young' soldiers come with the depth of knowledge of experience and age and must protect the human species from aliens.

Other books in the Old Man's War series:
The Ghost Brigades
The Sagan Diary
The Last Colony
Zoe's Tale
The Human Division

RED THUNDER • John Varley

Manny becomes friends with an ex-astronaut and his brain-damaged but intelligent cousin Jubal. They are all miffed that China is ahead in the race to the Red Mars. They come up with an unlikely machine that will help them beat the Chinese.

Other books in the Thunder and Lightning series:
Red Lightning
Rolling Thunder

THE DAY OF THE TRIFFIDS • John Wyndham

Bill Masen has been stung by triffids and therefore misses the spectacular meteor shower. When he removes his eye bandages he realizes that everyone who saw the meteor shower is blind. As he and Josella, a woman who also missed the shower, try to bring normalcy to the situation, the triffids begin to act up.

Other books by the author:
The Night of the Triffids
The Chrysalids

The Midwich Cuckoos
Chocky
The Kraken Wakes

MEET THE AUTHOR
POUL WILLIAM ANDERSON

Anderson was an American science fiction author who wrote several works of fantasy, historical novels and a great number of short stories. He received numerous awards for his writing—including seven Hugo awards and three Nebula awards—and was the sixth President of Science Fiction and Fantasy Authors of America as well as a founding member of the Society for Creative Anachronism.

In *The Boat of a Million Years*, ten immortals try to find someone like themselves and learn to keep quiet about their gift.

In *The High Crusade* it is 1345 and a huge alien spaceship lands in the little village of Ansby in Lincolnshire. Can the medieval army defeat the aliens?

Some of his other books are:
  Time Patrol
  Brain Wave
  Three Hearts and Three Lions
  The Boat of A Million Years
  The Broken Sword
  Trader to the Stars
  The High Crusade
  Future History of the Polesotechnic League series

WHERE LATE THE SWEET BIRDS SANG • Kate Wilhelm
The large Sumner family hides out in the Appalachian mountains in a post apocalyptic world. They decide to clone themselves so that in the future the clones will be able to breed properly and continue the species. But the experiment hits a snag.
Other books by the author:
   Barbara Holloway series
   The Deepest Water
   Constance and Charlie series

RINGWORLD • Larry Niven
Louis Wu wants to extend the celebration of his two hundredth birthday, therefore he begins to travel around the world, always ahead of the midnight line. He meets a Puppeteer, a Kzinti warrior and an unattractive girl Teela Brown, and together they go on a dangerous mission.
Other books by the author:
   The Borderland of Sol
   The Magic Goes Away

DELIRIUM • Lauren Oliver
There are ninety-five days left before Lena can undergo the invasive procedure that will cure her of the disease that killed her mother. This disease is love. By killing love America is safer from the madness and violence that love brings.
Other books in the Delirium series:
   Annabel
   Hana
   Pandemonium
   Raven

Requiem
Alex

THE ADORATION OF JENNA FOX • Mary Pearson

How far can parents go to save their child? When Jenna Fox wakes up from a coma, she does not remember her life and is told that she was in a a terrible accident a year ago.

Other books in the Jenna Fox Chronicles:
- The Rotten Beast
- The Fox Inheritance
- Fox Forever

Other books by the author:
- Scribbler of Dreams
- The Miles Between
- A Room on Lorelei Street
- Pickles in My Soup

ENDER'S GAME • Orson Scott Card

Is Andrew 'Ender' Wiggins the military answer to the Earth's problem? Ender is the result of some genetic experimentation. He has to be thrown out into the harsh environment to figure out if he will survive or perish against the alien enemy.

Other books in the Ender's Saga:

There are eleven novels, twelve short stories and forty-seven comic issues in the Ender saga. Some of these are:
- First Meetings in Ender's Universe
- Speaker for the Dead
- Xenocide
- Children of the Mind

THE MAN IN THE HIGH CASTLE • Philip K. Dick

What would happen if World War II had turned out differently? America is occupied by the Nazi Germans and the Japanese. Slavery is legal once again and the few Jews who survive hide under assumed names.

Other books by the author:
- Do Androids Dream of Electric Sheep?
- A Scanner Darkly
- Ubik
- VALIS

THE DISAPPEARANCE • Philip Wylie

What would happen if one fine day the world splits into two and one has only men and the other only women? What side would struggle and which one prosper? And would either of the worlds be complete?

Other books by the author:
- When Worlds Collide
- After Worlds Collide
- Gladiator

THE INCREDIBLE SHRINKING MAN • Richard Matheson

Scott Carey's life changes dramatically when he accidentally ingests some insecticide on a holiday. An exposure to a cloud of radioactive spray causes him to shrink by one seventh of an inch every day.

Other books by the author:
- I am Legend
- Hell House
- What Dreams May Come
- A Stir of Echoes

LORD OF LIGHT • Roger Zelazny

Earth is long gone and a group of men have made their home on another planet. Using the Hindu concept of reincarnation, their souls transmigrate to other humans and even animals. The 'Firsts' on the planet have superior powers and control the science of reincarnation. Then comes Mahasamatman, also known as Sam, Binder of Demons and Lord of Light.

Other books by the author:
 The Amber Chronicles

THE SIMOQIN PROPHECIES • Samit Basu

This is a breathtaking ride through a world peopled by different races and cultures across mythology and history. The Prophecies foretell the reawakening of the terrible rakshas, Danh-Gem, and the arrival of a hero to face him. As the day of Danh-Gem's rising draws closer and the chosen hero is sent on a quest, another young man learns of the difficult choices he must make in order to save the world from the rakshas.

Other books in the Gameworld trilogy:
 The Manticore's Secret
 The Unwaba Chronicles

Other books by the author:
 Turbulence
 Devi
 The Local Monsters

THE H-BOMB GIRL • Stephen Baxter

Laura carries a secret with her when she moves to Liverpool with her mother. Her father has given her a key and a code which she is to use if the end of the world is near. The Cuban Missile crisis looms large and the end of the world could be days away.

Other books by the author:
- Flood series
- Manifold series
- Ring
- Evolution

THE COLOUR OF MAGIC • Terry Pratchett

Rincewind, a wizard, is not a very happy man. He is expelled from the Unseen University because he has not learnt the most basic magic in his forty years there. Now he must act as a local guide for Twoflower, the Discworld's first tourist. When Ahnk Morpork is set on fire, the two are off for bigger adventures.

Other books in the Discworld series:

There are many books in the series, some of which are:
- The Light Fantastic
- Equal Rites
- Mort
- Sourcery
- Wyrd Sisters

MORE THAN HUMAN • Theodore Sturgeon

Six talented freaks come together to blesh—blend and mesh—their unique skills to be able to act as one organism and progress towards the next step in human evolution which is the homo gestalt.

Other books by the author:
- The Dreaming Jewels
- Venus Plus X
- Some of Your Blood
- Godbody

MEET THE AUTHOR
RAY BRADBURY

Bradbury was an American novelist, short story writer, essayist, playwright, screen writer and poet. He had a long, illustrious career in writing and won a number of prestigious awards including the Grand Master Award from the Science Fiction Writers of America, the PEN Centre USA West Lifetime Achievement Award and the Benjamin Franklin award.

The Martian Chronicles is a collection of stories of men leaving a destroyed Earth and making a life for themselves on Mars and the conflict between the native Martians and Earthlings.

Other books by the author:
  Fahrenheit 451
  The Illustrated Man
  Something Wicked This Way Comes

YOUR SCIENCE FICTION CHECKLIST

List down the books as you read them. Also rate them and share the ratings with your friends!

Rating scale
  Absolutely Smashing—4
  Very Good—3
  Strictly OK—2
  Did Not Like It One Bit—1

Read the Book	Rating

Supernatural and Horror

Who doesn't like a good scare—when it's within the pages of a book! Vampires, ghosts, strange creatures and things that go bump in the night. These books have all that and more.

LEVEL 1

THE SECRET PATH • Christopher Pike
Adam and his family move into Springville which should actually be called Spooksville. Strange things happen—a secret path that supposedly leads to other worlds, bugs crawling in Adam's house, and a tree that falls on Sally's house. What is going on?
Other books in the Spooksville series:
There are twenty-five books in the series, some of which are
- The Howling Ghost
- The Haunted Cave
- Aliens in the Sky
- The Cold People

REMEMBER ME • Christopher Pike
Shari Cooper remembers falling off her friend's balcony and wakes up dead. She has not committed suicide and is determined to find out who killed her and why.

Other books in the Remember Me series:
>   The Return
>   The Last Story

TRAVELLER'S GHOST • Deepa Agarwal
There is something strange about the photographer Yatri's house, thinks Kriti. Children are disappearing mysteriously and Kriti can feel the traveller's ghost too.
Other books by the author:
>   Anita and the Game of Shadows
>   Hunt for the Miracle Herb

THE HOUSE WITH THE CLOCK IN ITS WALLS • John Bellairs
Lewis goes to live with his small-time magician uncle after his parents die. The house is spooky because the walls are ticking.
Other books in the Lewis Barnavelt series:
There are twelve books in the series, some of which are:
>   The Figure in the Shadows
>   The Ghost in the Mirror
>   The Letter, the Witch and the Ring
>   The Doom of the Haunted Opera

THE GRAVEYARD BOOK • Neil Gaiman
Jack kills three members of a family and the fourth one, a toddler, escapes and crawls into a graveyard. He is adopted by a dead couple and called Nobody, or Bod. Bod is warned to not leave the graveyard ever, because Jack is still looking for him. Will he stay in the graveyard?
Other books by the author:
>   Coraline

Neverwhere
American Gods
Anansi Boys

THE GHOST OF THOMAS KEMPE • Penelope Lively
James is getting into trouble for things he has not done. Like writing strange things on fences, or dropping tea on the vicar's lap. But no one believes him in this new town.
Other books by the author:
Moon Tiger
How It All Began
Consequences
The Photograph

UNCANNY! • Paul Jennings
What happens when a family opens a magical chest? And have you heard of tattoos that come to life—long enough to find another resting place as their owner lies dying man. A collection of bizarre stories.
Other books by the author:
Unreal!
Unbelievable!
Round the Twist
Unmentionable!
Unbearable!

WELCOME TO DEAD HOUSE • R.L. Stine
Amanda and Josh's parents are delighted with the house in Dark Falls that Uncle Charlie has left for them. They move into the house, and the children are spooked. There are ghosts here that want to be friends forever.

Other books in the Goosebumps series:
There are many books in the series, some of which are:
- Stay Out of the Basement
- Monster Blood
- Say Cheese and Die!
- Welcome to Camp Nightmare
- Be Careful What You Wish For
- Why I'm Afraid of Bees
- The Scarecrow Walks at Midnight

THE PUFFIN BOOK OF SPOOKY GHOST STORIES • Various Authors

In this spine-chilling collection you will encounter a creepy spirit that occupies a deserted bungalow, the reincarnation of a goddess who wants the sacrifice of blood, an ominous swing that makes one fly far away into a dark, deathly world, and the sheer wrath of the dead. Read about a haunted school, a spooky wind-chime, a possessed doll and other supernatural elements.

LEVEL 2

THE THIEF OF ALWAYS • Clive Barker

Mr Hood's Holiday House has stood for a thousand years and is a pleasant place for fun and frolic. But something is not quite right and Harvey Swick is determined to find the truth about Mr Hood and his holiday home.

Other books by the author:
- Books of Blood
- The Great and Secret Show
- Cabal
- The Hellbound Heart

CIRQUE DU FREAK: A LIVING NIGHTMARE • Darren Shan
Darren goes to see the Cirque du Freak with his friend Steve. When a large spider, Madam Octa, stings Steve, Darren must become a vampire's assistant to save his friends's life.
Others in the Saga of Darren Shan:
- The Vampire's Assistant
- Tunnels of Blood
- The Vampire Mountain
- The Trials of Death
- The Vampire Prince

FEARLESS • Francine Pascall
Gaia Moore is fearless as she is born without the fear gene. Gaia sees her mother murdered in front of her, and her anti-terrorist mastermind father is in hiding.
Other books in the Fearless series:
There are many books in the Fearless series, some of which are
- Sam
- Run
- Twisted
- Kiss

THE YELLOW MAN • Hunter Laurenne
Michael Fischer leads an enviable life, until one night, a man in a yellow coat kills his family. Michael escapes, but the yellow man is on his trail, and from beyond their graves, his parents try to save their child.

THE CHANGEOVER • Margaret Mahy
Laura's brother is very sick. Her enemy has made his mark on her

and is sucking the life out of Laura's brother. She needs help and knows that Sorenson, the school prefect, is no ordinary person. He is a witch.

Other books by the author:
The Tricksters
BubbleTrouble
The Haunting
Alchemy

MEET THE AUTHOR
NEAL SHUSTERMAN

Shusterman grew up in Brooklyn where he began writing at an early age. He got his first book deal within a year of graduating from college. He is prolific and has written screenplays, TV scripts, movie scripts, music and stage plays.

In *Everlost*, Nick and Allie die in a car accident, but their souls don't go where they are supposed to. Instead, the children are caught in a limbo known as Everlost.

In *Full Tilt* brothers Blake and Quinn get into a bizarre roller-coaster park and they must complete seven rides before sunrise, else they will be trapped there forever. Blake soon realizes that each ride is a manifestation of his fears.

Some of his other works include the UnWind series and *The Schwa Was Here*.

SHADOWLAND • Meg Cabot

'Suze' Simon is a mediator. She can see and talk to ghosts. Most of them come to her when they have unresolved business with the living, and don't leave till it is resolved. So when Jesse, the ghost who haunts her room visits her, Suze is relieved, because she does not seem to want anything.

Other books in the Mediator series:
- Ninth Key
- Reunion
- Darkest Hour
- Haunted
- Twilight

MARKED • P.C. Cast

Sixteen-year-old Zoey Redbird gets 'Marked'—and she must change into an actual vampire or die. When she joins the House of Night, a boarding school for fledglings like her, she realizes that she has special powers.

Other books in the House of Night series:
- Betrayed
- Chosen
- Untamed
- Hunted
- Tempted

VAMPIRE ACADEMY • Richelle Mead

Three kinds of vampires exist in this world: the living Moroi, the undead Strigoi and Dhampirs, children of a Moroi and human or Dhampir. Lissa is a Moroi princess and her Dhampir friend Rose must protect her from the Strigoi.

Other books in the Vampire Academy series:
- Frostbite
- Shadow Kiss
- Blood Promise
- Spirit Bound
- Last Sacrifice

Other books by the author:
- Bloodlines series
- Georgina Kincaid series
- Dark Swan

TWILIGHT • Stephanie Meyer

Bella Swan is an ordinary mortal. When she moves to Forks, Washington, she is irresistibly drawn to the mysterious Edward Cullen, who is a vampire.

Other books in the Twilight series:
- New Moon
- Eclipse
- Breaking Dawn

TOM CLANCY'S NET FORCE EXPLORERS: CYPERSPY • Tom Clancy, Steve Pieczenik

A mysterious hacker has access to the 'wearable computer'. This allows him to get to the most private thoughts of any person. Net Force Explorer David must help his friends realize the potential dangers of these secrets reaching enemy spies.

Books in the Net Force Explorers series:

There are nearly eighteen books in the series, some of which are:
- Virtual Vandals
- The Deadliest Game
- One is the Loneliest Number
- The Ultimate Escape
- End Game

COYOTE MOON • Various Authors

Buffy is the Chosen One. She is destined to protect the human race from evil forces and demons. A usual night at the amusement

park turns into a nightmare when the shape shifters have fun of their own. Can Buffy save people from this horror?
Other books in the Buffy the Vampire series:
There are more than ninety books in the series, some of which are:
   Ghoul Trouble
   Prime Evil
   Resurrecting Ravana
   Child of the Hunt

THE BOY WHO COULDN'T DIE • William Sleator
Cherie Buttercup grants Ken a wish when his best friend dies in a plane crash. Ken gets immortality, but the price is his soul. When Ken realizes that his soul is being used as a zombie by Cherie, he wants to get his soul back.
Other books by the author:
   Interstellar Pig
   Parasite Pig
   The House of Stars
   The Green Futures of Tycho
   The Beasties

LEVEL 3

DRACULA • Bram Stoker
Jonathan Harker, an English solicitor, takes over a client, Count Dracula from his colleague who has gone insane. He travels to Transylvania to put the Count's affairs in order and is charmed by his host's graciousness. Soon he discovers that he is a prisoner in the castle and Dracula wants his fiancé Mina.

BLOODSUCKING FIENDS: A LOVE STORY • Christopher Moore

Jody does not want to be a vampire, but the decision is made for her. As she adjusts to her new nocturnal life, she meets Tommy, who knows the redhead will break his heart. And a showdowm awaits them at San Fransisco.

Other books in the Love Story series:
>   You Suck
>   Bite Me

OMEN • David Seltzer

Katherine and Jeremy Thorn are delighted as they are expecting a child. However, the baby is stillborn, and in order not to distress her, Jeremy agrees to replace the baby with another boy whose mother died at childbirth. Strange things begin to happen with Damien around.

THE PHANTOM OF THE OPERA • Gaston Leroux

The Phantom of the Opera lives under a famous opera house. He falls in love with Christine, a choir girl and teaches her beautiful music, thereby making her very famous. The Phantom loves Christine, but she loves another man…

Other books by the author:
>   The Mystery of the Yellow Room
>   The Secret of the Night

THE TURN OF THE SCREW • Henry James

A young governess goes to a country house to take care of two orphans. It is a pleasant house, but there seem to be dangers and ghosts lurking about.

Other books by the author:
- The Europeans
- Daisy Miller
- The Portrait of a Lady
- Washington Square
- The Bostonians

MEET THE AUTHOR
STEPHEN KING

King graduated from the University of Maine with a BA in English and sold his first short story, 'The Glass Floor' to Startling Mystery Stories in 1967. He also writes under the pen name of Richard Bachman and John Swithen.

In *The Shining*, Danny is only five years old, but he is a 'shiner', aglow with psychic voltage. When his father becomes caretaker of an old hotel, Danny's visions prove lethal for him. King has authored many books, some of which are:
- It
- Misery
- The Green Mile
- Carrie

THE CALL OF CTHULHU AND OTHER WEIRD STORIES • H.P. Lovecraft

This is a set of gripping tales of cosmic terror and insanity. In the Reanimator, Herbert West is the inventor of a solution that can bring back the dead. His experiments progressively become more bizarre, and then he tries to bring back to life his commanding officer.

GHOST STORIES OF AN ANTIQUARY • M.R. James

A collection of spooky ghost stories. Was there a room number 13 in the hotel? Does someone stay there? This and many more strange stories make this a delightful book.

ROALD DAHL'S BOOK OF GHOST STORIES

This collection has ghost stories by famous authors like J. Sherdian Le Fanu, Rosemary Timperley and L. P. Hartley. In the 'Upper Berth', try and figure out why passengers who sleep on that berth throw themselves off the ship. In 'Harry', why does a mother come to believe that her adopted child's playmate may not be imaginary after all?

MEET THE AUTHOR
WILLIAM SLEATOR

Sleator graduated from Harvard with BAs in music and English. His books have thrilled his readers and his works have been named among the best novels of the twentieth century by the Young Adult Library Services Association.

In the *Interstellar Pig*, Barney's boring seaside vacation suddenly becomes more interesting when the cottage next door is occupied by three exotic neighbours who are addicted to a game they call 'Interstellar Pig'.

Other books by the author:
- The Boy Who Reversed Himself
- Singularity
- The Boy Who Couldn't Die
- Marco's Millions series

YOUR SUPERNATURAL CHECKLIST

List down the books as you read them. Also rate them and share the ratings with your friends!

Rating scale
- Absolutely Smashing—4
- Very Good—3
- Strictly OK—2
- Did Not Like It One Bit—1

Read the Book	Rating

Traditional Tales

Each country has its own wealth of stories that have been passed on orally from generation to generation. These stories include folklore, religious tales, epics and legends. Here is a listing of some of the best such stories from India and around the world.

MEET THE BOOK
TALES OF ONE THOUSAND AND ONE NIGHTS
(ARABIAN NIGHTS)

The Persian King Shahryar is shocked to discover that his new bride is unfaithful to him and has her executed. Enraged, he begins to marry a succession of women only to execute each of them the next morning. Then he marries Scheherazade, who begins to tell him a tale but does not end it before dawn. The king is forced to postpone her execution because he wants to hear the end of the story. She finishes the tale the next night and then begins another one...this goes on for 1,001 nights!

The *Thousand and One Nights* is a collection of West and South Asian stories and folk tales. The work was collected over many centuries by various authors, translators and scholars, and the tales have their roots in ancient and medieval Arabic, Persian, Indian, Egyptian and Mesopotamian folklore and literature.

Some of the more famous tales from this collection are 'Ali Baba and the Forty Thieves', 'Aladdin's Wonderful Lamp' and the 'Seven Voyages of Sindbad the Sailor'.

LEVEL 1

RUSSIAN FAIRY TALES • Alexander Afanasyev
Afanasyev compiled more than 600 Russian tales and this collection has nearly 175 of them. From Baba Yaga the Swan Maiden to the glorious Firebird, this book has stories of kings and princesses, wizards and witches and enchanted children.

THE RAMAYANA FOR CHILDREN • Bulbul Sharma
A re-telling of one of the most famous Indian epic tales, the Ramayana, it tells us how and why Rama left the kingdom of Ayodhya and went into exile for fourteen years and what happened thereafter.
Other books by the author:
>   Tales of Fabled Beasts, Gods and Demons

ARMENIAN FOLK TALES AND FABLES • Charles Downing
Armenians had a great wealth of folk-tales. These were spun by simple people and narrated for entertainment in coffee houses or at home during the harsh winters.

MYTHOLOGY • Edith Hamilton
Edith Hamilton compiles myths and legends that have shaped Western culture. These include stories from the Greek, Roman and Norse mythology.
Other books by the author:
>   The Greek Way
>   The Roman Way
>   The Prophets of Israel

THE LITTLE BOOKROOM • Eleanor Farjeon
The author named this book after a little room in her childhood home which was full of books of all kinds and made the author's imagination run wild. In these twenty-seven stories, meet a flower without a name and a goldfish who wants to marry the moon and rule the world.

> ### MEET THE AUTHOR
> ### ANANT PAI
> Anant Pai, or Uncle Pai, as he was lovingly known, started the Amar Chitra Katha series of comics in an attempt to teach Indian children about their cultural heritage.
>
> Uncle Pai also founded *Tinkle* magazine, and created many of the notable characters who appeared in it.
>
> The contribution of Uncle Pai in engaging children in Indian mythology and folklore is unmatchable.

101 FOLKTALES FROM INDIA • Eunice De Souza
India has a wealth of folktales and this book brings together a lovely collection of them. From Kashmir to Nagaland and Assam to Kerala, these folktales carry a bit of flavour of everything!

POLISH FOLKLORE AND MYTH • Joanne Asala
A collection of popular Polish stories, including 'The Violin', 'The Legend of the North Wind', 'The Flaming Castle', 'The Village Dance' and 'The Unfinished Tune'. The book has been illustrated by the wycinanki (paper cutting) Polish-American artist, Alice Wadowski-Bak.

UNCLE REMUS • Joel Chandler Harris
Uncle Remus was a fictional African-American former slave who

told stories to children gathered around him. Br'er Rabbit is the main character in the stories. He plays tricks that catch others unaware.

FOUR ANCESTORS: STORIES, SONGS, AND POEMS FROM NATIVE NORTH AMERICA • Joseph Bruchac

A collection of traditional Native American tales categorised under the elements that make up the universe.

SEASONS OF SPLENDOUR: TALES, MYTHS AND LEGENDS OF INDIA • Madhur Jaffrey

The stories in this collection are arranged according to the Hindu calendar of festivals. There are anecdotes about the festivals and the folk tales that have grown out of these.

THE PUFFIN BOOK OF CLASSIC INDIAN TALES FOR CHILDREN • Meera Uberoi

A collection of tales from the Mahabharata, Ramayana, Panchatantra and traditional folklore of India.

THE KASHMIRI STORYTELLER • Ruskin Bond

A group of children gather around the Kashmiri storyteller every winter evening and he recounts stories from his land.

THE DRAGON'S SON • Sarah L. Thomson

The novel is narrated by four people in King Arthur's life and their part in Arthur's rise and fall as the King of England.

THE BROKEN TUSK: STORIES OF THE HINDU GOD GANESHA • Uma Krishnaswami

A collection of short stories on the myths and legends surrounding one of the best loved Hindu gods, Ganesha.

LEVEL 2

FOLKTALES FROM INDIA • A.K. Ramanujan
This compilation comprises of one hundred and ten tales translated from twenty-two Indian languages. Some of these are the Panchtantra and stories of Tenali Raman. Find stories on good and bad, ghosts and gods, jesters and storytellers and many others.

PUFFIN BOOK OF WORLD MYTHS AND LEGENDS • Anita Nair
Fantastic tales from across the world. What happens when the sky is too low and people keep bumping their heads against it? How did Mount Fuji become a volcano? And how did the snake get to shed its skin?

PUFFIN BOOK OF MAGICAL INDIAN MYTHS AND LEGENDS • Anita Nair
The most fantastic tales from Indian mythology retold accompanied by breathtaking colour illustrations by Atanu Roy.

THE GODMOTHER • Elizabeth Ann Scarborough
In Seattle, social worker Rose's wish comes true. And in comes fairy godmother Felicity Fortune, with silver hair and in strange clothes to save the city. But she has to use her magical powers carefully in the modern world.

Other books in the series:
 The Godmother's Apprentice
 The Godmother's Web

AESOP'S FABLES • Aesop
Aesop's Fables is a collection of fables credited to Aesop, a slave

and storyteller believed to have lived in ancient Greece between 620 and 560 BC.

FORBIDDEN FOREST: THE STORY OF LITTLE JOHN • Michael Cadnum

John Little tries to protect a lady when she is accused of murdering her husband. He becomes an outlaw, and in order to escape being captured, joins Robin Hood and his men in the Sherwood Forest.

INDIAN FOLK TALES AND LEGENDS • Pratibha Nath

A great collection of Indian myths and legends from all over the country. What happens when the Qazi of Jaunpur is mistaken for a donkey? And can Bhim match his strength against the mighty Hanuman?

INDIAN TALES • Romila Thapar

Sixteen stories compiled by India's leading historian. Read about the heros and heroines, gods and demons and the fight between the good and the evil.

A SKYFUL OF STORIES • Shobha Vishwanath

In the sky above, there are many constellations. How did they form? Of course there are scientific explanations for these, but there are many myths and legends from across the world too.

LEVEL 3

THE ILIAD • Homer

In the ninth year of the war between the Trojans and the Greeks, the Greeks realized that they may never win the war because Troy was still receiving aid from its vassals. While war raged on

Earth, the gods and goddesses were also divided in their loyalty. And Achilles, the greatest Greek warrior has a destiny to fulfil.

THE ODYSSEY • Homer

Odysseus was the King of Ithaca and one of the key players in the Greek Army in the war. After the fall of Troy, Odysseus began the long journey home. But it would be another ten years before he reached home to his wife Penelope.

THE STINKY CHEESE MAN AND OTHER FAIRLY STUPID TALES • Jon Scieszka

A funny take on fairy tales and characters. At the centre of the stories is Jack of the Beanstalk fame. The Little Red Hen, Chicken Licken and Goldilocks are here. The Stinky Cheese Man is the counter of The Gingerbread Man and Cinderrumplestiltskin combines the stories of Cinderella and Rumplestiltskin.

MEET THE AUTHOR
ELLEN DATLOW

Ellen Datlow has been an award-winning editor of short science fiction, fantasy, and horror for over twenty-five years.

Among the many anthologies she has compiled is the Retold Fairy Tales series. What happened to the dwarves after Snow White married the prince? And is Jack the only one who was right? Or did the Giant also have a story to tell? Books in the Retold Fairy Tales series are:

Swan Sister: Fairy Tales Retold

The Dark of the Woods

The mythic fiction anthology series presents original fiction exploring classic themes of myth and folklore from around the world.

> Other books in the series:
> The Faery Reel: Tales from the Twilight Realm
> The Coyote Road
> The Beastly Bride: Tales of the Animal People

THE PUFFIN MAHABHARATA • Namita Gokhale
A wonderful retelling of the story of the Mahabharata for young readers. It begins from the story of Devavrata who later became the great Bheeshma and weaves in many episodes that make this the world's longest epic in easy language.

THE ALCHEMIST: A FABLE ABOUT FOLLOWING YOUR DREAM • Paulo Coelho
Santiago travels from his homeland in Spain to the Eygptian desert in seach of a treasure buried among the Pyramids. Along the way he meets many people and realizes that 'treasure lies where your heart belongs'.

IN WORSHIP OF SHIVA • Shanta Rameshwar Rao
Hindu mythology is rich with stories—of kings and kingdoms, of gods and demons, of right and wrong, evil and good and love, loss and revenge. This is a collection of stories from Hindu mythology.

BEASTLY TALES FROM HERE AND THERE • Vikram Seth
Familiar characters in a new and magical form. How is that the Hare gets ignored after winning the race while the Tortoise becomes a celebrity? Of the ten tales here, two came from the 'land of Gup' to the author!

MEET THE AUTHOR
SAMHITA ARNI

Samhita started writing her version of the Mahabharata when she was barely eight years old. She also started illustrating each chapter. Her version, *Mahabharata: A Child's View*, was published when she was twelve.

Since then, the book has been translated and published in German, Italian, Spanish, French, Portuguese, Greek and Catalan.

She has written *Sita's Ramayana*, a graphic novel developed in collaboration with Patua artist Moyna Chitrakar.

YOUR TRADITIONAL TALES CHECKLIST

List down the books as you read them. Also rate them and share the ratings with your friends!

Rating scale
- Absolutely Smashing—4
- Very Good—3
- Strictly OK—2
- Did Not Like It One Bit—1

Read the Book	Rating

Books for Young Readers

This section is for all those parents and elder siblings who want to introduce the littlest ones in the family to the joy of books. Most of these are picture books or ones with almost equal amounts of text and illustrations—all the better to entice readers into the joy of leafing through books as early as possible! The world of picture books is a vast and fascinating place, and this is just a minute sampling of some of the best known ones available from Indian and foreign publishers.

HAROLD AND THE PURPLE CRAYON • Crockett Johnson

Four-year-old Harold can draw his own world. He wants to go for a walk in the moonlight but there is no moon, so he draws one—all with his purple crayon.

Some other books by the author:
- Harold's Fairy Tale
- Harold's Trip to the Sky
- Harold at the North Pole

THE VERY HUNGRY CATERPILLAR • Eric Carle

A caterpillar emerges from a cocoon and is so hungry that it eats many many things till it has a tummy ache!

Some other books by the author:
- Brown Bear, Brown Bear, What Do You See?
- 1, 2, 3 to the Zoo
- The Tiny Seed
- Do You Want to Be My Friend?
- The Mixed-Up Chameleon

IF YOU GIVE A MOUSE A COOKIE • Laura Numeroff, Felicia Bond

This is a delightful tale about what would happen if you gave a mouse a cookie. He would then want milk to eat the cookie with. Then he would want a straw to drink the milk with...

GOODNIGHT MOON • Margaret Wise Brown

One of the best bedtime books ever, this has a child saying goodnight to everything around before finally going to sleep.

WHERE THE WILD THINGS ARE • Maurice Sendak

Naughty Max is sent to his bedroom and it transforms into a jungle. There he meets all sorts of wild things and becomes their king before returning to his bedroom to a hot supper!

THE GIVING TREE • Shel Silverstein

About a boy and an apple tree and how the tree gives the boy everything he needs in his life from childhood to old age—shelter, fruits, its branches, its trunk and finally its stump to rest against.

THE LITTLE ENGINE THAT COULD

The book has gone through several editions with different authors and illustrators. It's a story of determination as a small engine hauls a long train over the mountain when the larger engines give up.

HOW DO DINOSAURS SAY GOODNIGHT? • Jane Yolen

A classic bedtime book, this one asks how dinosaurs behave when they have to go to bed. Do they throw tantrums and refuse to sleep? Or do they say goodnight politely and close their eyes?

HORTON HEARS A WHO • Dr Seuss

'A person's a person, no matter how small.' Horton the elephant must save the small person in the speck of dust, which is actually the planet of Whoville.

Some other books by the author:
- The Cat in the Hat
- The Cat in the Hat Comes Back
- Green Eggs and Ham
- Hop on Pop
- One Fish Two Fish
- Fox in Socks

THE TALE OF PETER RABBIT • Beatrix Potter

Peter Rabbit is very naughty and has been running around the garden all morning, getting into mischief and being chased by Farmer McGregor. When he returns home with his new clothes in tatters, his mother puts him to bed and makes him drink chamomile tea!

Other books by the author:
- The Tale of Squirrel Nutkin
- The Tailor of Gloucester

ANIMALIA • Graeme Base

An alliterative alphabet book, this has an animal for each alphabet along with a short poem and a number of illustrations for the animal. The author has also hidden his picture as a boy in each page!

ROOM ON THE BROOM • Julia Donaldson, Axel Scheffler

The witch and her cat fly happily till a stormy wind blows away the witch's hat, bow and wand. They are retrieved by a dog, a bird and a frog, and each animal asks for a ride on the broom. Is there room on the broom for all?

Some other books by the author:
- The Gruffalo
- Tabby McTat
- What the Ladybug Heard
- Tiddler

LADYBIRD READ IT YOURSELF SERIES 1 2 AND 3

Ladybird's celebrated classic series features traditional stories retold and designed so that children can read them for themselves. The sets are graded into four reading levels and are ideal supporting readers as they are built around high frequency (key) words. There is lots of repetition and the stories are fun to read.

TIGER ON A TREE • Anushka Ravishankar, Pulak Biswas

Black and orange in colour, this is written in short verse, full of words children will love. A tiger, scared by a goat's bleat, gets stuck up a tree. The villagers catch him, but now what should they do with him?

TO MARKET! TO MARKET! • Anushka Ravishankar, Emanuele Scanziani

A girl is sent to the market but she keeps getting distracted by all the colours, noise, crowds, the sights and smells. In the end, she returns home empty-handed!

MY MOTHER'S SARI • Sandhya Rao, Nina Sabnani

There are so many things a child can do with a sari—curl up in its folds, run through them as they hang from the washing lines, be rocked to sleep in a sari hung from the ceiling and even use it to wipe a runny nose.

THE GLUM PEACOCK • Tabish Khair, Nilima Eriyat

The peacock is sad because he is too colourful! He wants to be a chic grey, so all the other birds borrow some colours from him. But then they point out that he is now looking rather dull. Who will help out the peacock now?

MOHINI AND THE DEMON • Shanta Rameshwar Rao, Pulak Chakravarti

Mohini takes on Bhasmasura, who can turn people into ash by just clapping over their heads. Courageous and determined, Mohini makes the demon do a dance and tricks him.

MISTER JEEJEEBHOY AND THE BIRDS • Anitha Balachandran

Two sisters, one very strange Aunt, and a flock of escaped birds... Magic and mayhem comes in unexpected shapes and sizes to one small corner of a very big city.

THE PUFFIN BOOK OF BEDTIME STORIES • Various Authors

A lavishly illustrated collection of eighteen stories that will delight any child tucked up in bed. Each story is different from the other and there are all sorts of animals, people and things that go bump in the night in this book.

MUKUND AND RIAZ • Nina Sabnani

Two friends grow up sharing everything. But events in the country force them to part ways and they end up miles apart. Mukund remembers his dear friend even years later, along with his parting gift.

THE WHY-WHY GIRL • Mahashweta Devi, Kaniyka Kini

Moyna is too busy with the chores at home to go to school. This does not dampen her curiosity about everything around her and keeps on asking questions—so many whys!

ICKY, YUCKY, MUCKY • Natasha Sharma, Anitha Balachandran

Maharaja Icky of Ikhtarpur is having trouble finding a bride. After all, who would want to marry someone who juggles rosogullas. What he really needs is…a miracle.

MR MEN AND LITTLE MISS SERIES • Roger Hargreaves

Little Miss Chatterbox is well…a chatterbox. And Mr Tickle gets tickled very easily. Mr Slow takes forever to do his tasks and Little Miss Busy is hyperactive. This collection of more than a hundred small books features a character with a dominant personality and drives home simple moral lessons.

Some books in the series:
Mr Mean
Mr Fussy
Mr Chatterbox
Little Miss Bossy
Little Miss Wise
Little Miss Curious

Read the Book	Rating

Evergreen Reads

Some books defy the constraints of categories of genre and age with their timelessness. In this list you will find titles that have been hailed as the greatest books ever written. Some you may have encountered in abridged forms. Do attempt to read at least some of these greats of English literature.

CRY, THE BELOVED COUNTRY • Alan Paton
Stephen and Jarvis come from the opposite ends of the social spectrum in South Africa. What happens when young blacks leave their villages and the strong tribal culture.

BRAVE NEW WORLD • Aldous Huxley
This is one of the most brilliant pieces of satire ever written. Centuries from now, Earth is at peace with a population controlled at under two billion and people die at sixty. People are decanted and raised in Hatcheries and Conditioning centres and are divided into five castes. All is not well though.

BLACK BEAUTY • Anna Sewell
Black Beauty is a handsome horse and starts his career as a carriage horse for a wealthy family. But when he gets hurt, he is no longer presentable and suffers at the hands of cruel owners and hard work. But he does his best to serve humans.

A CLOCKWORK ORANGE • Anthony Burgess
A vicious fifteen-year-old 'droog' Alex terrorizes the city's streets at night. The authorities decide to train him by treating him to aversion therapy. Every time Alex sees a violent movie, he suffers from a bout of extreme nausea. But is this treatment effective?

Other books by the author:
- The Wanting Seed
- Earthly Powers
- The Doctor is Sick
- Nothing Like the Sun
- A Dead Man in Deptford

TALES FROM SHAKESPEARE • Charles and Mary Lamb
Want to read Shakespeare but feel daunted by the language? This is a perfect book to acquaint yourself with Shakespeare and his amazing stories.

JANE EYRE • Charlotte Bronte
The tale of Jane Eyre who is troubled emotionally by her aunt and cousins and goes on to become a governess at Thornfield Hall. There she falls in love with her employer Rochester. But will he return her affections? And does he hide a dark secret?

MEET THE AUTHOR
CHARLES DICKENS
Charles Dickens was one of the most popular writers of his time and created some of the most memorable characters, including Scrooge, Fagin, Pip, Miss Havisham and Uriah Heep.

Oliver Twist is one of his best loved works. It is about an orphan, Oliver Twist and his adventures on the streets of London with the evil Fagin and other thieves.

Other books by Charles Dickens:
The Pickwick Papers
Nicholas Nickleby
Old Curiosity Shop
David Copperfield
A Tale of Two Cities
Bleak House
Great Expectations
A Christmas Carol

ETHAN FROME • Edith Wharton
Ethan falls in love with his wife's cousin Mattie, who comes to take care of his sick, hypochondriac wife Zeena. Zeena asks Mattie to leave, but a 'smash-up' occurs.

WUTHERING HEIGHTS • Emily Bronte
The haunting love story of Heathcliff and Catherine who meet when they are young. As time goes by they drift apart and when Catherine marries someone else, Heathcliff plans revenge.

ALL QUIET ON THE WESTERN FRONT • Erich Maria Remarque
Baumer is a young boy who enlists in the German army to fight in World War I. Through life in the trenches, training and time spent in the military hospital, Baumer tries to make sense of the war and its daily horrors.

THE OLD MAN AND THE SEA • Ernest Hemingway
Old Man Santiago is considered 'salao' or unlucky because he has not caught a single fish in the last eighty-four days. Then Santiago ventures deeper into the sea and has an epic struggle

with a marlin. The struggle leads Santiago to believe that no one is worthy of eating such a dignified fish.
Other books by the author:
- A Farewell to Arms
- The Snows of Kilimanjaro
- For Whom the Bell Tolls

THE GREAT GATSBY • F. Scott Fitzgerald
Gatsby throws wild parties at his Long Island mansion and all of New York comes to party there. But nobody knows who Gatsby is and where he comes from. Nick Callaway becomes friendly with Gatsby and realizes that his cousin Daisy Buchanan is the one Gatsby loves and wants.
Other books by the author:
- Tender is the Night
- The Short Stories
- This Side of Paradise

CRIME AND PUNISHMENT • Fyodor Dostoyevsky
Rodion, an impoverished ex-student, makes a plan to kill an unscrupulous pawnbroker for her money and sets into motion a chain of events that destroys him and his family.
Other books by the author:
- The Brothers Karamazov
- The Idiot

SILAS MARNER • George Eliot
Marner is framed for theft by his best friend and becomes a recluse, until an orphan comes into his life...
Other books by the author:
- Middlemarch

The Mill on the Floss

NINETEEN EIGHTY FOUR • George Orwell
The novel gave us words like thoughtcrime, doublethink and Big Brother and is of a world where everything you do or even think is monitored by Big Brother. Winston Smith works at Minitrue, revising history according to what the Party wants it to be. He keeps a diary of negative thoughts about the Party in a hidden alcove. But when his illicit affair with Julia is discovered, as is his diary, Winston's life changes completely.
Other books by the author:
   Animal Farm

TO KILL A MOCKINGBIRD • Harper Lee
Scout's father Atticus Finch decides to defend a black person, Tom, who is accused of raping a white woman. The Maycomb community disapproves of this, and Scout and her brother face taunts and jeers.

UNCLE TOM'S CABIN • Harriet Beecher Stowe
The author wrote this book as a response to the Fugitive Slave Act of 1850 and this book is considered to be one that contributed to the American Civil War. It vividly portrays the inhumanness with which blacks were treated as slaves.

MOBY DICK • Herman Melville
A wandering sailor Ishmael joins Ahab's ship. Many of the captain's orders do not make sense to him until Ishmael realizes that Ahab has only one purpose on this voyage— to seek out and kill the white sperm whale, Moby Dick.

MEET THE AUTHOR
EDGAR ALLAN POE

Poe was an American author, poet, editor and literary critic. He wrote fantastic tales of mystery and the macabre.

The Tell Tale Heart follows an unnamed narrator who insists on sanity after murdering an old man who he claims possessed a 'vulture eye'. The murder is carefully planned and executed and the body is hidden after dismembering it.

Poe has a large body of work and some of his other famous short stories are:

The Fall of the House of Usher
The Pit and the Pendulum
Hop Frog
The Black Cat
William Wilson

CATCHER IN THE RYE • J.D. Salinger

Holden Caulfield, a seventeen-year-old, has been expelled from school. Instead of heading back home straight away, he spends time in New York City. Through the book we realize the reasons for his alienation.

ALL CREATURES GREAT AND SMALL • James Herriot

James Herriot was a country vet and this is about the trials and tribulations in his daily life. From helping birth a calf to consoling a man who loses his treasured pet, the book has amazing vignettes of people and animals.

Other books by the author:

All Things Bright and Beautiful
All Things Wise and Wonderful
The Lord God Made Them All

PRIDE AND PREJUDICE • Jane Austen
Mrs Bennett has only one agenda in life—to get suitable husbands for her five eligible daughters. Her second daughter Elizabeth dislikes the aristocratic Darcy who she thinks is arrogant and proud.

Other books by the author:
- Sense and Sensibility
- Emma
- Persuasion
- Mansfield Park
- Northanger Abbey

HEART OF DARKNESS • Joseph Conrad
Marlow takes over as the captain of a Belgian ferry boat in Africa. He has to transport ivory downriver, but the covert operation that Marlow is involved in is to return Mr Kurtz, another ivory trader to civilization. Kurtz is both a god and a prisoner to the native Africans and Marlow must rescue him.

CATCH 22 • Joseph Heller
Yossarian wants out from the endless missions his commander has made him fly. He can claim insanity if he wants to quit, but being driven mad by fear is entirely rational, so he can't quit.

THE GRAPES OF WRATH • Joseph Steinbeck
During the great Depression, a family of sharecroppers, the Toads, are driven from their home by drought and changes in the agriculture industry. They set out for California, one of the thousands of Okies who want a life of dignity.

Other books by the author:
- Of Mice and Men

WAR AND PEACE • Leo Tolstoy
The years leading up to, and succeeding the Napoleonic invasion of Russia in 1812 had devastating effects on aristocracy as well as the other sections of Russian society. The novel traces the story of five aristocratic families against this backdrop.
Other books by the author:
- Anne Karenina

A WRINKLE IN TIME • Madeleine L'Engle
A strange person comes to the Mury household one stormy night. It is Mrs Whatsit, who has been blown off course while tessering. She takes the children on a planet ruled by IT, a giant evil brain, who holds Mr Mury captive.
Other books in the Times series:
- A Wind in the Door
- A Swiftly Tilting Planet
- Many Waters
- A Ring of Endless Light

FRANKENSTEIN • Mary Shelly
The thirst for knowledge can be destructive too. Two friends attempt to stretch the boundaries of their respective professions. Victor creates Frankenstein in the laboratory and Robert attempts to reach the North Pole. Both face disastrous consequences.

DON QUIXOTE • Miguel de Cervantes
A fifty-year-old man decides that he is Don Quixote, a knight who sets wrongs right. He recruits his uneducated neighbour Sancho as his squire and embarks on a quest to make the world a better place.

UNTOUCHABLE • Mulk Raj Anand
The story of a single day in the life of Bakha, a toilet cleaner who accidentally bumps into a person of higher caste.
Other books by the author:
The Village
Across the Black Waters
The Sword and the Sickle
Coolie
The Private Life of an Indian Prince

THE SCARLET LETTER • Nathaniel Hawthorne
In seventeenth-century Boston, Hester Prynne is interrogated, found guilty and made to wear the sign of 'A' on her chest. 'A' stands for adultery and and she is considered immoral because she has had a baby from an illicit love affair, and nobody knows who the man is. But is she, as the woman, the only guilty party?
Other books by the author:
The House of the Seven Gables

THE PIGMAN • Paul Zindel
John and Lorraine befriend a lonely old man when they play a telephone prank on him. They decide to have a wild party in his house when he is recovering from a heart attack and realize that some betrayals are unpardonable.

THE GOOD EARTH • Pearl S. Buck
Wang-Lung gets married to unattractive O-Lan, a slave at the House of Hwang. Together they work hard and come to own the lands owned previously by the nobility. When he becomes prosperous, Wang-Lung betrays his wife by taking a concubine.

Other books by the author:
The Big Wave
A House Divided

NATIVE SON • Richard Wright
Twenty-year-old Bigger Thomas, an African-American, lives in utter poverty in a Chicago ghetto, but he takes up neither religion nor alcohol to make his existence easier. When he is accused of the murder of a young woman, he knows the outcome of the investigation.

THE CHOCOLATE WAR • Robert Cormier
Jerry is directed by the school bullies, the Vigils, to not sell chocolates during the annual chocolate sale. The acting headmaster Leon is livid as he has overspent the school's budget on chocolates and needs to see them sold, else he will lose his job.
Other books in the series:
Beyond the Chocolate War

MEET THE AUTHOR
SALMAN RUSHDIE
Salman Rushdie is well-known British Indian novelist and essayist. His novel, *Midnight's Children*, was awarded the Booker Prize. The book follows the life of a child born at the stroke of midnight as India gained its Independence in 1947. He is endowed with special powers and a connection to other children born at the dawn of a new and tumultuous phase in India's history.
Salman Rushdie has written two books for children. *Haroun and the Sea of Stories* is about Rashid Khalifa, the master storyteller whose skill deserts him when his wife leaves him

for a neighbour. Haroun must help his father.

In *Luka and the Fire of Life*, we meet Haroun's younger brother Luka who must wake up his father Rashid Khalifa, the legendary storyteller of Kahani, from his deep sleep.

WALK TWO MOONS • Sharon Creech

Sal travels to Idaho with her grandparents and she hopes to get her mother back, who has recently left her and her father. Sal tells her grandparents about her friend Phoebe who has disappeared, and as Sal narrates her story, she learns more about Phoebe, her own mother and herself.

Other books by the author:
- Love That Dog
- Ruby Holler
- Chasing Redbird
- Heartbeat

OF HUMAN BONDAGE • Somerset Maugham

The story of club-footed orphan Philip who leads a colourful life before settling down.

Other books by the author:
- The Razor's Edge
- The Painted Veil
- Cakes and Ale

THE RED BADGE OF COURAGE • Stephen Crane

Henry Fleming, a private in the Union Army, deserts his regiment in war, but comes back to realize that his comrades think he has been missing and injured in a fight. Henry now decides to fight to the best of his ability.

THE ONCE AND FUTURE KING • T.H. White
The epic of King Arthur, his magical Camelot and the various characters who shaped his destiny.

TESS OF THE D'UBERVILLES • Thomas Hardy
Tess is a young girl and is seduced by Alec. She is ridiculed because she gets pregnant and loses her baby. Later, she meets Angel who she loves with all her heart. But when she tells Angel about her past, he decides to separate from her to re-assess the situation. Then Alec walks back into her life.
Other books by the author:
- Far From the Madding Crowd
- Jude the Obscure
- The Mayor of Casterbridge

BELOVED • Toni Morrison
Sethe is a former plantation slave who now lives in a haunted home with her daughter Denver. When a fellow slave Paul exorcises the house ghost, a twenty-year-old girl lands up at their doorstep. She has no marks on her palms and her clothes and shoes do not indicate she has travelled a great distance. Who is this young girl?

THE SOUND AND THE FURY • William Faulkner
The novel is a masterpiece. It takes the reader through the same story four times, through the eyes of four different people. And each narrative helps piece together the tragedy of the Compson family.
Other books by the author:
- As I Lay Dying
- Absalom! Absalom!
- Light in August

LORD OF THE FLIES • William Golding
A group of school boys survive a plane crash and are stranded on an island. What seems idyllic and fun soon deteriorates into violence, selfishness and cruelty.
Other books by the author:
> Pincher Martin
> Free Fall

MEET THE AUTHOR
RABINDRANATH TAGORE

Rabindranath Tagore was a prolific writer who wrote three thousand poems, two thousand songs, eight novels, forty volumes of essays and short stories and fifty plays. His major theme was humanity's search for God and truth. He was awarded the Nobel Prize in Literature for his collection of poems, *Gitanjali*.

'The Kabuliwallah' is a touching story of a man who leaves his country and comes to India to earn a living. He sells dry fruits and gets attached to a little girl Mini, who reminds him of his daughter back home.

Some other great works by Tagore include:
> The Hungry Stones
> The Land of Cards
> Gora
> The Home-Coming

YOUR CLASSICS CHECKLIST
List down the books as you read them. Also rate them and share the ratings with your friends!
Rating scale
> Absolutely Smashing—4

Very Good—3
Strictly OK—2
Did Not Like It One Bit—1

Read the Book	Rating

Made in the USA
Monee, IL
03 May 2026

49438687R00142